Chinatown Jeet Kune Do

ESSENTIAL ELEMENTS OF BRUCE LEE'S MARTIAL ART

Tim Tackett and Bob Bremer

Chinatown Jeet Kune Do

ESSENTIAL ELEMENTS OF BRUCE LEE'S MARTIAL ART

Tim Tackett and Bob Bremer

Edited by Sarah Dzida, Raymond Horwitz,
Jeannine Santiago and Jon Sattler

Graphic Design by John Bodine

Photography by Rick Hustead and Thomas Sanders

Models: Shawn King, Jeremy Lynch and Jim Sewell

Printed in the United States of America
Library of Congress Catalog Number: 2007941888
ISBN 10: 0-89750-163-2
ISBN 13: 978-0-89750-163-7

First Printing 2008

WARNING

BLACK BELT BOOKS
A Division of **OHARA** **▯** **PUBLICATIONS, INC.**
World Leader in Martial Arts Publications

Dedications and Acknowledgments

I dedicate this book to Bruce Lee with the utmost respect.

—*Bob Bremer*

To my wife Geraldine:

Thanks for 47 wonderful years.

—*Tim Tackett*

We also give a big "thank you" to the following students who helped out by posing for the photos in the book:

Jim Sewell—a first-generation *jeet kune do* student
Jeremy Lynch—a second-generation jeet kune do student
Shawn King—a second-generation jeet kune do student

—*Tim Tackett and*
Bob Bremer

Foreword

Today, only a handful of people in the world have studied *jeet kune do* under my husband, Bruce Lee. Bob Bremer is one such student, and we are fortunate to have his recollections of Bruce's teachings recorded in this volume. In the 40-plus years that I have known Bob, his legendary status among JKD practitioners is well-deserved. To my knowledge, Bob has always strived to pass on only the techniques and aspects of Bruce Lee that he himself experienced without branching out, elaborating, embroidering on or interpreting anything beyond Bruce's teaching. I respect Bob's approach to teaching jeet kune do, for Bruce had much to offer that did not require updating, revising or adapting. With Bob Bremer, you get the real deal.

Tim Tackett was among the first of the second-generation students, and I have known him nearly as long as Bob. Throughout the years he has studied jeet kune do, Tim has also had a well-respected career as a high-school teacher, drama coach and published writer. Together with Bob, they have been passing on Bruce's art of JKD in Tim's garage to small groups of privileged students. This practice harkens back to Bruce's beginnings in the early '60s, when he taught his art to only a few friends for no compensation. In the '70s, this was continued during Tim's first years of jeet kune do training in the original "backyard" group, and the tradition still exists in Tim and Bob's Wednesday Night Group.

It is of utmost importance that the thoughts and recollections of Bruce's original students are recorded for the benefit of martial artists who are interested in jeet kune do teachings because they come directly from Bruce Lee. I appreciate the time, effort and primarily the love that Bob and Tim have put into transcribing their experiences. With the publication of this book, the art and philosophy of Bruce Lee will be preserved for the benefit of generations to come.

Today, Bob Bremer and Tim Tackett serve on the advisory committee of the Bruce Lee Foundation. For more information about the Bruce Lee Foundation, please visit www.bruceleefoundation.com.

— Linda Lee Cadwell

About the Authors

Tim Tackett

In 1962, Tim Tackett's martial arts training began when the U.S. Air Force sent him and his family to Taipei, Taiwan. While there, Tackett trained in kung fu. When he returned with his family to California a few years later, Tackett opened a kung fu school. However, he was also surprised to discover that he was one of the few non-Chinese kung fu teachers in America.

Tackett first saw Bruce Lee in 1967 at Ed Parker's International Karate Tournament. He decided then and there to study *jeet kune do*. Unfortunately, Tackett wasn't able to begin JKD training until after Lee's Chinatown school had officially closed. To fill the void, Dan Inosanto ran classes from the gym in his backyard. When Tackett joined the backyard class in 1971, there were only about 10 students in the class. Today, those students make up the who's who of modern jeet kune do.

Bob Bremer

In 1967, Bob Bremer saw Bruce Lee demonstrate *jeet kune do* and became one of the first people to enroll in the Chinatown school, missing only one class in three years. Bremer brought a no-nonsense approach to fighting, earning him the title "No. 1 Chinatown ass kicker" from Dan Inosanto. As a result, Lee invited him to his house on Sundays for one-on-one training sessions. After Lee closed his school, Bremer became part of the original backyard class taught by Inosanto. In the 1980s, he began attending Tim Tackett's Wednesday Night Group classes, where his firsthand experience with Lee changed the way the group approached jeet kune do.

About the Wednesday Night Group

After training under Dan Inosanto for four years, Tim Tackett asked him whether he could share what he had learned from him with other people. By this time, Tackett was finding it harder to teach kung fu because he thought *jeet kune do* was much more efficient. When Inosanto told him that he could teach jeet kune do but not to the general public, Tackett closed his school and started teaching a group in his garage every Wednesday night. He kept the class small and charged nothing for the lessons. This group became and still is called the Wednesday Night Group.

Bob Bremer began attending the Wednesday Night Group in the 1980s, and what he shared was illuminating. Because of his private lessons with Bruce Lee, Bremer was able to go into great detail about how to make a technique work and how to strike at the correct range. Bremer also went into detail about certain principles, like the water hose, whip and hammer. In regards to the hammer principle, he taught the group how Lee used it as a means to strike with nonintention. Bremer also shared how Lee explained to him that the best way to win a fight was to simply reach over and knock an opponent out, to get rid of passive defensive moves and intercept an opponent's attack with enough power to immediately end the fight. Because of Bremer's participation, the Wednesday Night Group threw away inefficient techniques.

This instruction also helped Tackett notice that Lee had taught different things to different people. For example, Bremer was a big guy whose natural inclination was to crash the line and blast his opponent, and Lee accommodated that inclination in their private lessons. In contrast, Lee taught people with smaller builds, like Ted Wong, to rely on footwork to be elusive. And while both approaches are valuable, Bremer and Tackett understood that most JKD stylists retained what naturally worked best for them, which is the way Lee wanted JKD practitioners to learn. This method tends to benefit students more than a set curriculum, but it can be difficult for teachers because they are naturally inclined to fight a certain way, meaning they may not be aware that their style isn't necessarily the best for everyone. (The Wednesday Night Group eventually came to believe that JKD practitioners should not be clones of their teachers.) Instead, the student, while adhering to the basic principles of jeet kune do set by Lee, should still try to attain a unique expression of the art.

In the 1990s, Jim Sewell, another former Chinatown student, joined the Wednesday Night Group, bringing the same no-nonsense approach to fighting as Bremer had. Today, Sewell, Bremer and Tackett run the group together with the same basic approach to learning, which is that all techniques must work against a skilled fighter. Of course, many techniques work against an unskilled fighter, but the question is whether it will work against a seasoned street fighter, a skilled boxer, a classically trained Thai fighter, an experienced grappler or a JKD practitioner. If it doesn't work against any of those opponents, why bother learning it?

If you are interested in learning more about the Wednesday Night Group, please visit www.jkdwednite.com. Or to discuss jeet kune do, visit the *Black Belt* forums at www.blackbeltmag.com/interactive.

Table of Contents

Introduction

Jeet kune do confuses many martial artists because it is a combat system that was still evolving when Bruce Lee died. It is also unlike other traditional martial arts because Lee used his personal experiences and knowledge to develop what many now consider to be the most successful method of self-defense. To properly explain this evolution, however, we need to start at the very beginning in Hong Kong.

Although Lee was born in the United States, he grew up in Hong Kong, where he studied *wing chun* kung fu under master Yip Man at age 13. While there, Lee learned the *chi sao* energy drill, numerous self-defense techniques and 40 of the 108 wooden-dummy techniques. However, before he could learn the entire wing chun system, Lee's parents sent him abroad. At the time, it was common for kung fu schools and students to challenge each other to fights, and Lee fought in several feuds. As a result, Lee's parents sent their hotblooded, 18-year old son back to the United States so he couldn't participate in future challenges.

At 19, Lee began teaching a modified version of wing chun to a handful of students in Seattle, partly because he wanted to have people with whom he could work out and partly because he wanted an arena in which to test moves. It was a modified version most likely because Lee did not learn everything before leaving Hong Kong. This left room for Lee to incorporate his fascination with other arts into his classes by teaching students techniques from other systems, like the inverted kick from the praying mantis style of kung fu, into his classes. His methods proved successful, and Lee opened his first kung fu school in 1962 with his good friend and student Taky Kimura. Because Lee's Chinese name is Lee Jun Fan, his school was named the Jun Fan Gung Fu Institute. The name also described exactly what the school taught: Bruce Lee's style of kung fu.

1964 was a pivotal year for Lee. He married the love of his life and moved his new family to Oakland, California, to open his second kung fu school and be near his friend James Lee. Bruce Lee also did a demonstration at Ed Parker's Long Beach International Karate Tournament. During the demonstration, Lee caught the eye of Jay Sebring, the hairstylist of William Dozier, who was the producer of the television show *Batman*. Sebring brought the young martial artist to Dozier's attention, which led to a screen test for a televised Charlie

Chan spinoff called *Number One Son*. The project died, but ABC eventually offered Lee the part of Kato in a TV series called *The Green Hornet*. The series exposed the American public to Lee and kung fu. Following the show's cancellation after one season, Lee supported his family by offering private lessons to several actors he met through the show, including Steve McQueen and James Coburn.

Also in 1964, a fight radically changed Lee's understanding of the martial arts. Traditionally, kung fu teachers in the United States did not pass on the art to non-Chinese students. Lee, however, believed kung fu should be available to anyone, regardless of their background, so he admitted non-Chinese students into his school. This enraged the other members of the San Francisco kung fu community, which is why they sent a Chinatown kung fu practitioner to challenge Lee to a fight with the following stipulation: If Lee accepted the fight and lost, he would either have to quit teaching kung fu to non-Chinese students or close down his school.

Lee won the fight, but he wasn't satisfied with his performance. He began to seriously research classical fighting systems from both Europe and Asia, becoming one of the first people to blend Eastern and Western arts together. Lee believed that traditional martial arts bound a fighter to the dictates of that style's defense and offense, whereas a truly proficient fighter needed to be able to deal with opponents from any combat background. This was why Lee was so interested in martial arts beyond kung fu. He wanted to understand the techniques and principles of these arts so he could develop the necessary tools to handle them.

During the 1960s, Lee's ideas were revolutionary especially because style was king. If you were a Japanese or Korean karate student, you spent your time practicing with and against that style only. In fact, the only time you saw practitioners from various Chinese, Japanese and Korean styles together was when they competed against each other at tournaments like Ed Parker's. Competitors could look at any martial artist and immediately tell what style he practiced because of his stance and movements. In addition to this, the tournaments were non-contact, which meant competitors would train without learning how to absorb an attack, and Lee thought that this was an unrealistic way to practice and compete.

Lee's exploration of European and Western martial arts gave him a new appreciation for realistic fighting, especially in regards to Western boxing. After the San Francisco fight, he started experimenting with boxing techniques and principles he picked up from books and films. He decided to mix the sport's techniques and footwork with his developing style in order to increase his mobility and give him a larger arsenal of strikes.

Lee also realized that many martial artists relied too much on the passive defense of blocking. A time lag existed between the block and the eventual counterattack, which would often give an opponent the chance to attack again before the defender could counter. The disadvantage became even more apparent if an opponent faked an attack. However, it was from his research into Western fencing that Lee realized that feinting opened a window of opportunity between the opponent's attempt to block the "false attack" and the opponent's next strike. This broken rhythm of attack became one of jeet kune do's main principles.

Most important of all, Lee concluded that an effective self-defense system must be simple.

His research showed him that most martial arts had too many responses to deal with a single form of attack. In fact, he found that some martial arts contain more than 20 ways to deal with a particular punch, which could be confusing during a real fight rather than one simple and direct solution.

This was why Lee particularly liked the idea of a simultaneous block and hit because it simplified countering. He first learned about the concept in wing chun and then integrated it with "stop-hitting," a counterattack method found in Western fencing that required the practitioner to lead with his dominant hand. By standing with his strong hand and leg forward, Lee found that he could do "Western fencing without the sword," so he implemented stop-hitting into his empty-hand system.

During this time, Lee worked constantly to get the most power from his tools. While working on *The Green Hornet* and opening his third kung fu school in the Los Angeles Chinatown area with his assistant and partner Dan Inosanto, he refined his new style. In the end, Lee found that the best way to stop an opponent's attack was to intercept it with a stop-hit by his strong hand or leg. Consequently, in 1967 Lee named his martial art jeet kune do, which means "the way of the intercepting fist." By naming his art this, Lee established that intercepting an opponent's attack would be the main focus of any JKD practitioner.

For reasons that remain unclear, Lee closed his Los Angeles school in 1970 and told Inosanto to stop teaching jeet kune do to the general public. Some believe that Lee came to the conclusion that nothing in self-defense should be set in stone. Others think that Lee feared that some JKD practitioners would misuse his art. To explain his decision, Lee said to Bob Bremer in a conversation: "If knowledge is power, why pass it on indiscriminately?" Whatever the case, Inosanto only taught JKD to a select group of Chinatown students in a gym he built in his backyard; Bob Bremer was one of those students.

In the meantime, Lee moved back to Hong Kong in 1971 to film the action movie *The Big Boss*. After the film became a hit in Asia, Lee remained in Hong Kong where he continued to make movies until he passed away on July 20, 1973, while filming *Game of Death*. He was 32 years old.

———— ✿ ————

Following Lee's death, jeet kune do became one of the best known but least understood martial arts. Many people curious about JKD ask:

- Is it merely doing your own thing?
- Is it adding anything that suits you from as many different martial arts as possible?
- How does the structure that Lee taught in Los Angeles differ from what he taught in Seattle? If it is different, how is it different?
- What part of the old wing chun structure still fits in with the structure that Lee taught in Los Angeles?
- Is there really a JKD structure? If yes, what is it?

In addition to this, even though Lee is considered a pioneer of what we now call "mixed martial arts," we think that it gives a false impression of what he was really trying to accomplish when he created JKD. When we look at the mixed martial arts of today, we usually think of Thai boxing, Western boxing and various grappling systems that are "mixed" together from ring sports. To call JKD a mixed martial art incorrectly suggests that Lee brought together various arts and called what was created "jeet kune do." It is true to say that Lee investigated many systems, but he was looking for the universal truth that lies within any martial art; he didn't just borrow a punch from one or a kick from the other. For instance, Lee may have added certain punches and training methods from boxing, but jeet kune do is not boxing because it is not based on the idea that a minor punch, like a jab, is the setup for a major blow. Also, while JKD may take some combat theory from Western fencing, it is far from just fencing with the front hand. In actuality, what Lee did for martial arts is more akin to what Albert Einstein did for science. Einstein read many books on physics, studying the ways of the masters who had gone before him. However, having gained all that knowledge, he came up with an original idea, and this is the truth of all professions: Students study the work of the past and then they create a new idea, which is what we believe Lee did when he created jeet kune do.

And even though no one can know for certain what jeet kune do would look like if Lee was still alive, we can still share what he taught. This is why the book focuses on Lee's final years of teaching and chronicles his final recorded developments of JKD. It is also an introduction to what Lee taught at the Los Angeles Chinatown school as well as what Bremer learned during his one-on-one lessons at Lee's home. In addition to that, we've both been fortunate enough to train with Inosanto and observe Lee during demonstrations. Simply put, *Chinatown Jeet Kune Do: Essential Elements of Bruce Lee's Martial Art* shows readers how to make jeet kune do principles work in combat.

Part I
Basic Principles

A Note to Readers

The keys to *jeet kune do* are speed, flow, deception, simplicity, sensitivity and power. While these concepts are easy to understand, it takes a lot of work to use them efficiently in combat. We recommend that readers experiment with the forms presented in this book because even Bruce Lee would tailor his techniques to suit the different physiques and abilities of his students. To do this, ask yourself the following questions while reading:

- How do I use what I'm learning in a combat situation?
- Even though I may be able to perform the move, is it deceptive/fast/simple/etc. enough?
- Is my technique powerful/deceptive/sensitive/etc. enough to do what it was designed to do?

The first part of the book explains the basic foundation of jeet kune do. It begins with JKD's fighting stances because stances are the cornerstone of any martial art, and jeet kune do's stances are unique because they favor speed and mobility over strength and solidity. Chapter 2 discusses how to control the distance between yourself and an opponent, and the final chapters in Part 1 focus on how to develop powerful punches and kicks. The book also includes a glossary in the back with specific martial arts terms and jeet kune do definitions.

Chapter 1
STANCES

"The art of *jeet kune do* is simply to simplify."

—Bruce Lee, *Tao of Jeet Kune Do*

Western fencing defines the fighting measure as the optimum and ideal distance for a fencer to be from his opponent. To maintain this critical distance, a fencer strives to stay just beyond the reach of the opponent's longest weapon, which refers to a sword. Similarly, *jeet kune do* defines the fighting measure as just beyond the reach of an opponent's longest weapon, but there is one difference. Instead of a sword, the longest weapon refers to an opponent's stationary finger jab, which can vary from opponent to opponent. However, no matter who the adversary is, a JKD practitioner always stands in one of two basic stances—the natural or the fighting stance—in order to easily move in and out of the fighting measure.

The Natural Stance

The first basic stance is the natural stance, which helps JKD practitioners not only prepare for attacks but also deceive their opponents into thinking they are not threats. They do this because many people, when confronted, make the big mistake of immediately jumping into a fighting stance, which rarely frightens a potential attacker and makes it easier for him to justify using a weapon. However, appearing unskilled and submissive may trick the opponent into not taking the fight seriously, which makes it easier for the JKD practitioner to counter and intercept his attacks.

The Natural Stance

A: A *jeet kune do* stylist (left) looks harmless in his natural stance.

B: The exact positioning of the natural stance differs depending on a JKD practitioner's body type and personal preference.

The Fighting Stance

The second stance is called the fighting stance, and there are two versions available for JKD practitioners. The first is the toe-to-arch stance, which is the more mobile of the two and allows the JKD stylist to move in any direction at any time. The second fighting stance is the toe-to-heel stance, which is not as mobile as the toe-to-arch stance but gives the JKD practitioner a more stable base from which to launch and block attacks.

To do the toe-to-arch stance properly, place your weight on the balls of your feet and stand with both heels raised slightly above the ground as if there is a layer of dust between the heels and the ground. Although it can feel awkward at first, with pratice you'll be able to move faster in any direction. To avoid being knocked off-balance, position your rear heel at a 45-degree angle and your front foot at a 25- to 30-degree angle. By keeping your front foot slightly straighter than the rear foot, your front hip will more easily swing toward your target, making all your punches more powerful.

To do the toe-to-heel stance correctly, position and angle your feet like in the toe-to-arch stance but with two main differences. First, place your feet a little wider apart to create a more stable base. Second, keep your front foot flat on the floor as a stabilizer.

Toe-to-Arch Stance

A: When his feet are positioned properly, a straight line should run from the toes of a JKD practitioner's front foot to the arch of his rear foot.

Toe-to-Heel Stance

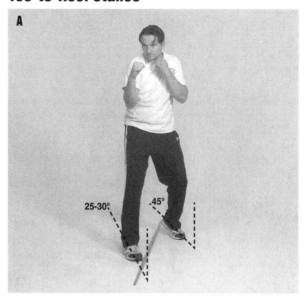

A: The stick shows how a straight line should connect the front edge of a JKD stylist's lead foot to the heel of his rear foot in the toe-to-heel stance.

Both fighting stances work during a conflict, so which stance a JKD practitioner uses depends on his specific body type, personality and the circumstances he finds himself in. For example, if he is facing a very large opponent, the mobile toe-to-arch stance is probably the best choice for the situation. In contrast, the toe-to-heel stance may be better if the JKD stylist prefers to finish the fight quickly with a strong starting offense.

Remember, jeet kune do requires a constant balance and trade-off between power, distance, speed and safety, so experiment with the stances—as you would with any JKD technique—to see which one works best for you. There is no hard-and-fast rule for when to use a particular stance. And because intercepting an attack requires speed, try to learn to flow quickly and naturally from one fighting stance or technique to another.

Balance and Mobility

When jeet kune do stylists stand in a fighting stance, they generally position their feet at least shoulder-width apart for optimum balance. Of course, the toe-to-heel stance will always be slightly wider than the toe-to-arch stance, but the distance between the two feet positions should be the same regardless of the stance chosen or the distance from an opponent. Basically, if your front foot is too far forward or your rear foot is too far back, you will lack mobility and be easier to knock off-balance. In addition, your groin will be exposed if your feet are too far apart, which leaves you vulnerable to immobilizing attacks.

Proper Position

A: JKD practitioner Jeremy Lynch stands in a fighting stance with his feet in the correct position and his weight properly distributed.

B: Notice that his lead foot is not too far forward and that his rear foot is not too far back. Instead, Lynch is perfectly balanced to deal with any attack.

Improper Positions

A: The stick shows that Jeremy Lynch's feet are too far apart, leaving him vulnerable to a groin attack.

B: Because he's hunched over and his feet are too close together, Lynch's body is off-balance, and he is in danger of being knocked over by an opponent.

In regards to weight distribution, a JKD stylist tries to place about 65 percent of his weight on the rear foot and 35 percent on the front foot to help propel his hand strikes forward at a greater speed. However, don't worry about being exact. Instead, it's more important for you to know that you should place less weight on your front foot. If you do put half or more of your weight on your front foot, you will need to transfer that weight to your back leg before you can launch a lead hand-strike or stop-kick attack. The noticeable transfer of weight will instantly telegraph your intent to your opponent, helping him avoid or intercept your attack. That's why it important for JKD stylists to hamper their front lead foot as little as possible because, in doing so, they will only increase their speed and ease in executing techniques.

Also, remember to pay attention to the position of your heels. If you quickly push off on a raised rear heel, your entire body should shoot forward like a runner coming out of a starting block. Because of this quick thrust, your raised rear heel drives your fist forward with greater power and speed, and it adds to your agility because it allows you to perform faster footwork. In addition to this, the raised heel acts like a shock absorber, which will allow you to "roll" or "rock" back when avoiding a punch.

Stance Strength

A: Jeremy Lynch tests his stance to see whether it is too narrow or wide by having a partner push him.

B: When shoved, Lynch loses his balance because his stance is too narrow. However, because his rear heel was raised, he should easily "rock" back into his original stance.

In regards to the front heel, a JKD stylist raises it during a punch because it will transfer some of his body weight from the front foot to the front leg. With even less weight on his front foot, the stylist now has a little "give" if he is punched. This means that because he hasn't transferred all his body weight to the back leg, his rear foot is easier to move in case he needs to retreat. The JKD stylist also increases his mobility, spring and ability to absorb blows by bending his knees slightly in both fighting stances.

Improper Balance

A: Jeremy Lynch takes a lead step forward but is off-balance because his step puts most of his weight onto his front foot. Now he is unable to recover his fighting stance quickly enough, and his wide stance makes him vulnerable to attacks.

Proper Balance

A: At the fighting measure, Jeremy Lynch should be able to step forward at least 12 inches and remain balanced while hitting his opponent with his front hand.

B: Lynch takes a lead step out and back but remains balanced because he is in the proper fighting stance.

Posture

Even though it may make a stylist's posture look poor, hunching is the correct way to stand in jeet kune do. This is because it makes a JKD practitioner a smaller target to hit and allows him to uncoil with the speed of a cobra to reach his own target.

To hunch correctly, hold your arms in front of your face and draw your shoulders up to protect your chin and vulnerable midsection. If you let your shoulders drop or don't keep

Improper Posture

A: Because his shoulders are too far back, Jeremy Lynch limits the use of his rear leg and arm to attack. It will take more time for him to make contact with his target if he uses them.

Proper Posture

A: With his shoulders properly hunched, Jeremy Lynch can protect his face and midsection. He is also a smaller target.

B: Here, Lynch hunches his shoulders properly. Note the width and length of Lynch's stance.

them level and straightforward, it will be harder to rotate your hips, shoulders and body when throwing a straight lead punch. However, if your opponent can't reach you, it's OK to relax your shoulders.

Strong Hands, Strong Stance

Because jeet kune do is based on the idea that the most efficient defense is an interception, Bruce Lee realized that leading with the strong hand is the best way to do this. The strong hand refers to a person's dominant side, which in most people is the right side, but left-handed people should lead with their left hand. However, no matter which side is dominant, it's crucial for a JKD practitioner to keep his strong hand forward in the fighting stance because that determines how quickly he intercepts an attack.

To understand why it's better to stop an attack with the strong hand, use a stick or imagine that you are holding a sword. Your weapon is your defense; before your opponent can hurt you, he must penetrate it. If the stick is in your rear hand, your weapon will have to travel a greater distance to intercept an attack. In contrast, the lead hand will always be there to act as a barrier or weapon. (Because of the distance it has to travel to reach the opponent, the rear hand actually generates more power, which makes it a more useful follow-up weapon.)

Stick Test

A: Shawn King (left) and Jeremy Lynch face each other in proper fighting stances. The stick illustrates how the lead hand is like a weapon because it is always between the two fighters.

B: King and Lynch face off with their strong hands forward and without sticks for reference. However, notice that if either opponent moves in to attack, the other will have an immediate defense.

C: Properly balanced, Lynch throws a punch with his strong hand. Notice how difficult it is for King to intercept, avoid or get around the attack. If Lynch used his rear hand to attack instead, King would have had more time to block the strike.

How a JKD practitioner holds his hands depends on the distance between him and his opponent. To help students understand this concept, some JKD teachers divide distance into four ranges: kicking, striking, trapping and grappling. These divisions often confuse students because many attacks work at all these ranges. For instance, the trapping range places a JKD martial artist close enough to grab his opponent's arms, but he can still perform a scoop kick to the groin at this distance. Furthermore, although the kicking range is supposedly outside of the hand-striking range, the martial artist can still perform a push-step finger jab to the opponent's eyes from this distance.

To simplify things, Lee divided the distance between two opponents into three ranges: long, medium and close. For example, when at long range—which is a safe distance from any opponent, meaning the JKD stylist is beyond the fighting measure—it's OK for him to keep his hands low. In contrast, if the stylist is at close range, meaning in the brim-of-fire line (See Page 23.), it's safer for him to keep his hands high. Even though a stylist can perform most JKD techniques at any range, many work better when performed at a specific distance. For example, while a JKD practitioner performs a hand attack at long range, a kick at that distance may actually be more efficient for him. However, Lee did provide some general guidelines. At midrange, for example, Lee taught that lead- and straight-rear punches or a JKD blast (See Page 45.) are most effective. At close range, in contrast, Lee taught that the most useful techniques are bent-arm punches, knee or elbow strikes, or trapping techniques. (Note: This book does not show knee and elbow strikes, but it does address close-range attacks.)

Also, remember your hands' positions. The front hand, which is mainly used for attacking, should directly point at your opponent's nose. The rear hand, which is primarily used for blocking, is positioned near the left side of the chin, ready to deflect any blow. To find the proper position, imagine that your front hand is a gun that is ready to fire as soon as your opponent attacks. If your gun is pointed at the ground, you will have to raise it up to shoot and stop your attacker. Instead, it is far more efficient to have your gun pointed at the target. One way to ensure that you get the best hand position is to raise your arms over your head and then drop them. They will fall naturally into the close-range ready position.

Proper Hand Position

A: Bob Bremer demonstrates how to drop his hands into the proper position while in the fighting stance.

B: Like a gun, his fists are aimed at his opponent's nose.

In regards to his arms, a JKD practitioner keeps his front arm about one fist away from his body and his elbows tucked into his sides. There are three reasons why he tucks in his elbows: First, it helps him put maximum power into his punch. You wouldn't keep your elbows out while pushing a car or bench-pressing, would you? So why would you want your elbows out when you punch? Second, it helps disguise the JKD stylist's intended attack. If he punched with his elbow out, his opponent would see the oncoming attack more easily. By keeping his elbow in, the JKD stylist not only produces a more powerful punch but also makes it harder for his opponent to see the intended strike. Third, it helps protect his ribs. When hunched over with his arms in front of him and his elbows in, the JKD practitioner can block strikes and kicks to his midsection with greater ease.

Improper Arm Position

A, B, C: Jeremy Lynch incorrectly throws a straight lead punch with his elbow out. Notice how easy it is to see the punch extend.

Proper Arm Position

A, B, C: Jeremy Lynch correctly throws a straight lead punch with his elbow in. Notice how difficult it is to see the punch extend.

In many photos, Lee is in a fighting stance with his front arm low or even resting on the front of his thigh. This again has to do with distance because Lee knew it wasn't efficient to keep his arm raised, especially if he was outside his opponent's attacking range. Basically, Lee understood that if his opponent couldn't punch him, there was no need to wear himself out by holding his fists up for protection. Likewise, by keeping his hand low, Lee improved his balance while moving because it made his stance more solid. This becomes apparent if you try moving with your hands high and then with your hands low—you'll realize that having your hands low will make you more stable. In addition, Lee found that the low hand position could fake out his opponent by tricking him into launching a hand attack because the adversary would think Lee was closer to him than he really was. This way, Lee was able to "draw" the opponent's attack in the direction of his choice before intercepting it with stop-kick or hit. However, note that if you want to keep your lead hand low at close range, you must have a great sense of distance and upper-body evasion skills like Lee. Don't be too confident because judging the correct distance may be difficult and could affect the effectiveness of your stance.

Improper Hand Height

A: Tim Tackett (left) faces off against Shawn King at what appears to be a safe distance.

B: Tackett attacks King with a finger slice. Because King's hands are too low, he can't defend himself quickly enough.

Proper Hand Height

A: When in doubt, keep your hands high because they will stop most attacks.

B: This time when Tim Tackett launches a finger slice, Shawn King easily blocks it.

Training

The lead foot is another important part of stances in jeet kune do. In most JKD classes, too much emphasis is placed on attacking or defending against an opponent who is in a matching stance, meaning each adversary has the same lead foot forward. While most experienced stylists will be in a left lead about 90 percent of the time, you can never be 100 percent certain. That's why you should make sure that you are able to defend against all kinds of opponents, regardless of whether they lead with their right or their left. In training, experiment and practice all the techniques from matching and unmatched stances.

Matching Stances

A, B: Jeremy Lynch and Tim Tackett (left in A) both lead with the same strong hand, placing them in matching stances.

Unmatched Stances

A, B: Tim Tackett (left in A) leads with his right leg because his right hand is his strong hand, but Jeremy Lynch leads with his left leg because his left hand is his strong hand or because he is a fighter, like a boxer or mixed martial artist, who places his strong hand in the rear instead. This places them in unmatched stances.

Chapter 2
FOOTWORK

"The essence of fighting is the art of moving."

—Bruce Lee, *Tao of Jeet Kune Do*

To have any chance of intercepting an attack, a JKD practitioner must control the distance between himself and his opponent through footwork. Footwork helps a JKD practitioner not only maintain the fighting measure but also avoid the brim-of-fire line, which is the distance his opponent can strike at him without having to move forward. If the opponent can hit the practitioner without needing to take a step forward, his attack will probably succeed because he doesn't need to use many movements. In fact, fencers often talk about the time lag that occurs from when they first see an incoming attack, to when they see where it's going and to when they must parry it. Most agree that if the opponent is fast, within striking range and attacks with little or no preparation—basically, he condenses the number of his movements—then the defender can't avoid the hit. That's why control over your footwork is so vital to success in combat; it can be the deciding factor between whose strike lands first.

Improper Distance

A: Jeremy Lynch (right) moves too close to Bob Bremer, entering the brim-of-fire line.

B: Because of his proximity, Bremer easily lands a finger jab to Lynch's face.

Proper Distance

A: Jeremy Lynch and Tim Tackett (right) are at the fighting measure, which is the proper, but critical, distance.

B: Lynch launches a finger jab but misses because Tackett is at the fighting measure rather than in the brim-of-fire line. Because Tackett controls the distance with footwork, Lynch will have to take another step forward to hit him.

Maintaining the Fighting Measure

In the toe-to-arch stance, the "step and step" is the footwork of choice to maintain the fighting measure because it aids mobility, but it can also be done in the toe-to-heel stance. To do it correctly, take a lead step by moving your front foot forward. Next, step forward with your rear foot so that when you've completed the movement, you are once again standing in a proper toe-to-arch stance. Some people may confuse this footwork as a step that slides, but it is performed with no sound and on the balls of your feet, which would be impossible to do if you slid. However, you still want your feet to stay as close to the ground as possible because your footwork should consist of quick, light and small steps.

The Step and Step Forward

A: Jeremy Lynch stands in the fighting stance.

B: He takes a step forward with his front foot.

C: To complete the move, the rear foot steps; it does not slide.

The Step and Step Backward

A: To step backward, Jeremy Lynch stands in a proper fighting stance.

B: He moves his rear foot back one step.

C: To complete the move, Lynch steps back with his front foot. Note: In combat, the steps should move more fluidly.

JKD practitioners also maintain the fighting measure with a "step and slide," which they can also perform in the toe-to-arch stance even though it complements the stronger base of the toe-to-heel stance. While the footwork may look similar to the step and step, it's quite different. Instead of stepping, slide your feet as if there was a layer of dust on the floor, keeping them as close to the ground as possible. As a result of doing this, your base remains more solid, making it harder for your opponent to knock you off-balance.

The Step and Slide

A: Jeremy Lynch performs the step and slide by sliding his lead foot a step forward.

B: To complete the move, Lynch slides the rear foot up. He does not step.

There is other footwork available to maintain the fighting measure. In the "side step," for instance, a JKD practitioner sidesteps an opponent in order to maintain the fighting measure and keep his adversary in front of him. Unlike the circular pivot discussed on Page 28, the side step is a lateral movement.

The Side Step

A, B, C: To sidestep to the right in a right-foot lead, Jeremy Lynch moves his right foot first and then follows quickly with his left foot.

D, E, F: To sidestep to the left in a right-foot lead, Lynch slides his left foot to the left and follows quickly with his right.

If an opponent were to get behind a JKD practitioner or dance around him by circling, the practitioner would keep his adversary in line by pivoting. By doing this, a JKD practitioner not only stays in front of his opponent but also conserves energy because pivoting requires little movement.

The easiest way to pivot left or right is by sliding your rear leg as much as possible. By sliding your rear leg rather than your lead leg, you maintain your balance and keep your tools (hands and feet) pointed at your opponent so you'll be ready to respond to any attack.

Pivoting

A: To pivot to the left, Jeremy Lynch slides his back foot out and counterclockwise. He then circles it around to his new position while pivoting on his front leg.

B: When his pivot is complete, Lynch's feet and stance mirror his original but from a different position.

Ultimately with any footwork, you are trying to keep your opponent in front of your hands instead of allowing him to move around or behind you, out of the fighting measure. To practice footwork, like the step-and-step or the step-and-slide, have a training partner start in the fighting measure and then move toward and away from you. Your job during this exercise is to maintain the fighting measure by not letting him get too close or too far away.

Training

Because it is essential to maintain the fighting measure, JKD teachers always stress footwork to their students. However, it seems that when students practice their footwork, they often make the same errors. One such mistake is moving the same distance every time with their lead foot. To train effectively, JKD practitioners should vary how far they step, which makes their footwork more natural and combat ready.

For instance, some students step forward two inches with the front foot and then two inches with the rear, while other students step six inches forward with the front foot and six inches with the rear. Neither movement is incorrect because the students are correctly trying to keep their feet the same distance from each other after each step to maintain their fighting stance. However, to ensure that they do this, most students never vary the distance they step and incorrectly train with the same rhythm; for example, every three seconds they will step forward or back. In reality, a JKD stylist wants to constantly vary his movements' rhythm in training to prepare for realistic combat. The length and width between his feet remain the same, but the distance and timing he uses to move doesn't have to be constant from step to step. This is called "broken rhythm."

In addition, the rest of the techniques in this book can be used with either the toe-to-arch or toe-to-heel stance. When learning a technique, experiment with both stances to see which one will work best for you. You can even combine the two stances by placing your rear foot halfway between where you would normally position your toe and arch. If you stand in the fighting stance and draw a line from your front lead toe to your rear heel and from your front lead toe to your rear arch, the in-between measurement, which is about three inches, is where you would place your foot. Remember to use whichever stance works best at that particular moment to execute a technique correctly.

Chapter 3
HAND TOOLS

"The best way to win the fight is to just reach over and knock him out."
—Bruce Lee, as remembered in conversation by Bob Bremer

Lee designed jeet kune do to work this way: When an opponent attacks, a JKD practitioner picks up on his intention and intercepts his attack with enough power to disable him by using the strong, lead hand to do a stop-hit. While the concept seems simple, it's very difficult to pull off during a real fight, which is why so many JKD practitioners lead with their nondominant hand or throw weak punches when they lead with their dominant one. A common reason they do this is because some JKD practitioners also train in other martial arts like Western or Thai boxing. In the case of the former, Western boxers lead with their nondominant hand to launch a weaker punch, like a jab, to set up a stronger punch, like a cross. In the case of the latter, Thai fighters use their nondominant leg to maximize the distance and power of their main kicking tool—the round kick—and this puts their nondominant hand in front. However, in jeet kune do, Lee decided that having the strong hand forward is not only the best way to intercept an attack but also the quickest way to end a fight, which is why this philosophy plays an important role in this chapter.

Punch Power

Before we discuss how to punch properly, let's first examine what can inhibit a hand tool's power. When a JKD practitioner launches a punch, his hip should point and swing toward his opponent. By doing this, he ensures that his hips channel the power and momentum of his entire body into his fist both before and after the impact. When the practitioner transfers his weight from his front leg to the rear one, his hips and momentum will tend to go where his front foot is pointed. If he doesn't point his foot—and therefore hip—correctly, he would have instead sent his fist in one direction and body in another direction.

In addition to this, a JKD practitioner tries not to lock his front knee while transferring his weight between his feet because it weakens his punch. A straight leg hinders the power that is transferred from the movement of the legs into the strike. As an added danger, his knee could be broken if his opponent launched an unexpected side kick.

Improper Hip Movement

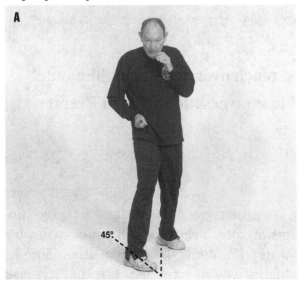

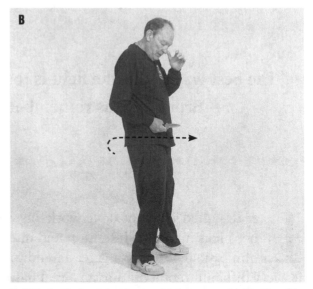

A: Tim Tackett stands with a dagger on his hip and with his front foot at a 45-degree angle in the fighting stance. While a dagger clearly demonstrates the angle and movement of the hip for this punch, using a stick is just as valid.

B: If Tackett's front foot is at a 45-degree angle, his hip will not go toward the target, making his punch weaker. Notice how Tackett's knife moves to the side.

Proper Hip Movement

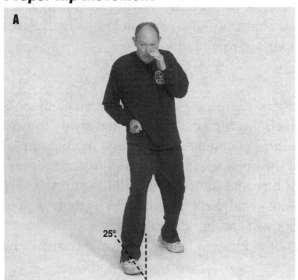

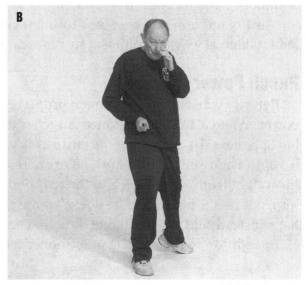

A: If the front foot is at a 25-degree angle, it is easier to finish the thrust with the power generated by a hip transfer.

B: Because it's harder for an opponent to notice the transfer of power, Tim Tackett's attack is much more deceptive. Notice how a subtle twist of the rear foot also helps Tackett's hip movement.

Improper Hip Movement and Interception

A: Tim Tackett (right) faces Jeremy Lynch, and they are both armed with knives. Unfortunately, Tackett's foot is angled at a 45-degree angle.

B: When both fighters strike, Tackett's hip rotation moves his entire body into the opponent's strike, leading to potentially fatal consequences.

Proper Hip Movement and Interception

A: This time, Tim Tackett's front foot is at a better angle.

B: When he transfers his weight from the rear to front leg, Tackett's body follows the straighter line of his thrust. This helps him avoid Jeremy Lynch's knife strike and take advantage of the opponent's open centerline.

To generate enough power to properly finish an opponent with a punch, use your whole body, not just your arm. Remember that the power from a JKD stylist's stationary punch comes from transferring the weight from his rear leg to the front leg by quickly twisting his rear foot. (See Page 32.) Unlike the front foot, the rear foot should be pointed at a 45-degree angle to help facilitate movement. If the stylist's rear foot is flat and straight, it won't help the JKD practitioner twist his hips or propel his weight from one leg to another. Simply put, more weight transfer simply translates into a means for more power.

In addition, a JKD practitioner does not overextend his center of gravity too far over his front knee when transferring his weight. This is because overextending leaves him vulnerable to a counterattack because the practitioner is now unbalanced and unable to recover quickly to throw another punch. One way to check whether you are transferring your weight correctly is by locking your elbow and placing your palm on your training partner's chest. Lee called this the "no-inch punch." With your arm straight out to show overextension, your push will lack significant power unless you properly transfer your weight.

No-Inch Punch

A: Tim Tackett puts his hand on the chest of his training partner with his elbow locked to show the influence weight transfer has on his punch's power.

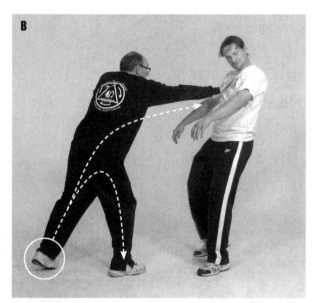

B: Transferring his weight from his rear leg to his front leg, Tackett pushes his opponent away with significant power.

In addition to the rotation of the body, punching power also comes from speed. To avoid being blocked or countered, a JKD practitioner needs his rear-hand strike to be faster than a lead-hand strike because it must travel farther to reach the target. In fact, Lee taught his students that a punch should "penetrate" (follow through) at least two inches beyond the target to extend the distance and generate more power. However, if a JKD stylist's punch penetrates more than the recommended two inches, his attack will be more like a push than a strike. This not only increases his chances of a hand injury but also makes it more difficult for him to quickly recover his original stance and counter with a second punch or kick.

To generate the necessary speed for an effective punch, snap your elbow as your arm extends. This not only increases speed but also increases the punch's power. Make sure that your elbow is fully extended when your fist makes contact with its target, which is two inches behind the point of impact. While some instructors may think that by fully extending your arm you can break it, Lee taught his students that their punches should be so fast and potent that an opponent can't block it, let alone break it. To show his students how to snap their elbows quickly and correctly, Lee taught them to practice their punches with 1-pound weights in each hand. Once you are able to deliver straight punches with the proper two-inch penetration, practice them at every range.

Elbow-Snap Exercise (See Application on Page 38.)

A: To snap his elbow, Bob Bremer uses a 1-pound weight.

B: He holds his hands in a ready fighting stance and quickly thrusts his fist forward until his elbow is extended; then he snaps it back.

Power and Distance

Because a punch's power also comes from snapping the elbow, a JKD practitioner needs to be able to instantly judge how much of his body to use while punching. Ideally, he would be able to use all his power when he strikes, but we do not live in an ideal world. Many times, opponents stand either too close or too far from the other to launch an attack from the ideal range. When this happens, a JKD practitioner moves either himself or his opponent to get the optimum distance. Sometimes, he may need to step back and punch. Other times, the stylist may need to hit at his opponent with a push-step. No matter the method, however, the success of the JKD practitioner's attack as well as its power depends on his ability to judge the proper distance in a split second.

Penetration at a Distance

A: Tim Tackett (right) and Jeremy Lynch are both beyond the fighting measure, but Tackett intends to launch a strike anyway.

B: For his strike to penetrate beyond the impact point, Tackett extends his shoulder as he swings his hip. A step forward also adds to his penetration power.

If you're too far from your opponent to take a lead step but close enough to consider an attack, launch a straight punch with a push-step. A good way to gauge the distance is to assume that it's easiest to score with a "push-step strike" from one to two feet outside of the fighting measure. When performing a finger jab, start your attack an additional two inches away to compensate for the attack's additional reach. It's difficult to land any punch with a push-step at long range unless you have spent a lot of time practicing. Lee, for instance, practiced this strike with Bob Bremer from six feet away. Before attacking, Lee would ask Bremer whether he felt safe. The moment after Bremer would say "yes," Lee would smack him hard on the forehead.

Push-Step Strike

A: Before launching his attack, Jeremy Lynch stands in a fighting stance.

B: Lynch pushes off with his rear leg to close the distance between him and his opponent.

C: The strike fully extends when Lynch's front foot lands on the ground.

D: To recover his original position, he pushes in the opposite direction with his front foot.

E: Lynch is back in an on-guard position.

Sometimes, you are too close to your opponent to generate power from your torso or legs. To prepare for these situations, build up arm strength and endurance through focus-mitt training. By hitting the focus gloves from every range, you will build up so much strength that you no longer need to worry about whether you're at the proper distance. While this may sound easy, it is difficult to do because you need to generate the same power using only your arm.

Elbow Snap

A: Bob Bremer (right) is so close to Jeremy Lynch that he can only use his arm to punch; he needs to snap his elbow to build up enough power for his attack.

B: Bremer's body barely moves, but Lynch is still forced back because Bremer successfully "snapped" his arm with enough force.

Deception

Even though a punch's true power begins in the rear foot, the lead hand should move before the rest of the body because it is a more deceptive movement. From the rear foot, a JKD practitioner shifts his weight while swinging his hips to transfer energy up through his body and out through his fist, but this is something his opponent will definitely see. However, by moving his lead hand first, a split second before he transfers his weight, the JKD practitioner masks his attack behind a small movement that the opponent won't see until it's too late.

Basically, if your hand attack is on its way to the target before your opponent sees it, the odds of hitting him are much greater than if you started the punch by moving your entire body. In addition, a fast push off from the rear foot will only compound the speed and power of your strike. Because a JKD practitioner's punch should hit the target just before his front foot touches the ground, his transferred weight only adds extra power to the strike's execution.

To maintain the lead hand's deception, relax as much as possible because tensing your muscles not only signals your intent to your opponent but also slows your strike. In addition to this, don't close your fist until just before the moment of impact because it will keep your flexor muscles relaxed until the last possible second, thus maximizing your snap. Remember, the dynamics in moving the lead hand before the lead foot are incredibly difficult to learn, so persevere in and be patient with your training. Also, note that all this applies to a punch as well as the finger jab.

Full-Body Strike

A: Even a finger jab begins at the rear foot.

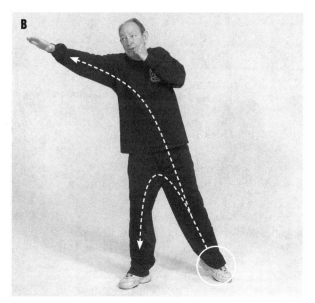

B: Here, Tim Tackett demonstrates how to strike with his whole body.

Fists

There are three main ways to make a fist for striking—vertical, horizontal and diagonal— and they all have their uses. For many JKD practitioners, the horizontal fist is the weakest because it doesn't absorb as much impact force and might move them backward. Lee also found that the diagonal fist is slightly stronger than the vertical fist because of how it aligns the bones in the hand with the bones in the arm. From experience, you'll learn that certain techniques work better with certain fist positions. For example, a straight punch to the body seems to work best with a horizontal fist, while a hook punch seems more effective with a vertical fist. The best way to determine the structure of a punch, however, is by extending your arm with your elbow locked. Experiment with a training partner by punching his palm using the three kinds of fists.

Fists

A: horizontal fist

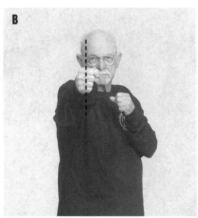

B: vertical fist

C: While most JKD practitioners perform a straight lead punch with a vertical fist, Bruce Lee told Bob Bremer to punch with his hand at a 45-degree, or diagonal, angle. This helps line up the bones in the arm. Note: Hit your opponent with your middle knuckles, which lessens the chance of self-injury.

The Straight Lead Punch

Because it's the best way to successfully intercept an attack, the straight lead punch is the most important hand tool in JKD, which is why practitioners spend the most time working on it. In fact, this was the main reason Lee chose to put his strong hand forward—a straight lead punch needs optimal power. While most unarmed opponents tend to lead with their dominant hand, even if it is in the rear, Lee took the idea from Western fencers—who always hold their sword in their front hand—that the strong hand should be forward.

When attacking with a straight lead punch from the fighting measure, take a lead step with your lead foot to bridge the gap because it is probably the fastest way to execute the attack. But first, swing your front hand to hide your intent. Then, quickly step out with your lead foot just enough so that your punch makes contact two inches before your arm is fully extended. While it may look like you are merely stepping out with your front foot, you are really thrusting it forward with a hard push off from your rear leg. The timing should be such that your hit lands a split second before your lead foot returns to the ground, which adds to the strike's speed and deception.

However, it takes a lot of practice to get the most out of this punch because you need to be able to judge the correct distance in a split second. Improve your timing and judgment by training with a partner who's wearing focus mitts. The partner flashes the glove at various angles. Following each move, practice punching it with speed and power. Repeat this exercise from various distances within the fighting measure, ranging from a quarter inch to as long as you can take a lead step and recover your original position.

Straight Lead Punch/Finger Jab

A: Shawn King adopts a fighting stance. He can either strike with his fist or fingers. In this case, he will do a straight lead finger jab.

B: King initiates the straight lead finger jab by moving his hand first before he transfers his weight. It's a slight movement, which makes it harder for his opponent to read how he will attack.

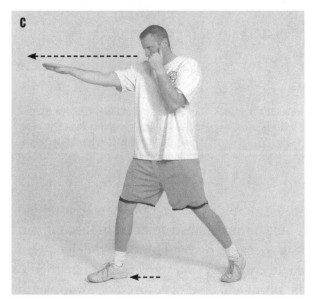

C: The straight lead finger jab is a direct forward strike, which is also the case for a straight lead punch.

D: Without losing balance, King recovers his original fighting stance.

While the straight lead punch or finger jab is the preferred hand tool in jeet kune do, sometimes it's better to attack an opponent at an angle. As a result, jeet kune do includes the curved straight lead punch, which—as the name implies—is a lead punch that goes around an opponent's centerline. This makes the curved straight lead punch a good way to intercept a straight-line attack because a JKD practitioner can move either to an open inside or outside line. In addition, most people practice blocking punches that come straight on, so an angled attack offers the element of surprise.

The mechanics of the curved straight lead punch are basically the same as the push-step. Start the strike with your strong hand, then push forward at an angle to the right with your rear leg. Once your front foot touches the ground, step with your rear leg to the right. The front hand, front leg and rear leg should move so fast that it looks like one movement. Ideally, the attack will hit just before your front foot lands on the floor. When executing the punch, move fluidly rather than in separate steps. Don't think of the smaller movements as 1, 2 and 3. Instead, think of them as a 1A, 1B and 1C.

Curved Right Straight Lead Punch in a Matched Lead

A: Jim Sewell and Jeremy Lynch (right) face each other in matching stances with their strong hands forward.

B: Lynch begins the curved attack with his hand, and his body follows.

C: Lynch steps out first with his front leg and follows with his rear. After the strike, both of his feet are back in the fighting stance.

The curved straight lead punch helps a JKD practitioner avoid an opponent's stop-hit or punch whether they are facing each other in matching or unmatched stances. In the matching stance, the JKD practitioner has an added advantage because his lead foot will finish between his opponent's legs, giving him a chance to strike at the adversary's groin. The opponent is also left in a vulnerable follow-up position in the unmatched stance, too. For example, the opponent is in a left lead stance while the JKD practitioner is in a right lead stance. After the practitioner strikes, the opponent will still have a strong base. However, he can only use his lead hand to defend himself from a follow-up strike because his rear hand will be too far away to help.

Curved Right Straight Lead Punch in an Unmatched Lead

BLOCK

A: When facing Jeremy Lynch in an unmatched lead, Tim Tackett (right) still can execute a curved attack. Despite having a stronger base, Lynch can only defend one side.

B: Tackett blocks Lynch's left jab with his left arm while striking with a curved straight lead punch.

There are other variations of the straight lead punch available for JKD stylists that use the same ideas of movement and balance. One such example is the straight rear punch, which is sometimes called a cross, like in boxing. However, the two are different punches because the boxing cross is used for when a boxer needs to slip inside an opponent's punch or to "cross" over the opponent's arm to hit him. In contrast, the jeet kune do straight rear punch does not cross the opponent's punch.

The Cross in Western Boxing

A: Coming from behind and around Shawn King's (left) arm, Jeremy Lynch "crosses" it and strikes at his target. This is technically a cross.

Straight Rear Punch

A: What most people misconstrue as a cross is actually a straight rear punch. Tim Tackett (left) slips inside Jeremy Lynch's strike and hits his chin straight on. His arm naturally negates his opponent's attack.

The straight rear punch should be performed with the same elbow snap and two-inch penetration as the straight lead punch. Because the punch by itself is too easy for an opponent to counter, a JKD practitioner usually uses it as a follow-up to the straight lead punch. For example, as soon as your lead hand returns to its original on-guard position, use the pistonlike action of your arms to follow up with the straight rear punch. If your straight lead punch hits your opponent's chin or nose, his head will snap back, making it harder for you to reach him with the follow-up straight rear punch. To remedy the situation, take a small step with your rear foot so that your straight lead punch will make contact with its target. Whether or not you have to "cheat up" with a small step, always rotate your front heel while twisting your waist. This transfers energy from the rear leg to the front and throws your lead shoulder forward, which channels power through the fist. At the end of the punch's execution, your rear foot and hip should be pointed at your target.

The step-back straight lead punch is another variation of the straight lead punch, which a JKD practitioner uses when he is too close to an opponent to step in and hit him with enough power to end the fight. Instead, he will step back and then punch him. To do this, push back and off with your front foot to propel your body backward. This movement is the exact opposite of the forward motion of a straight lead punch. While moving backward, aim at a point two inches behind the target of impact. To achieve enough power, push off with your front foot hard and fast. In fact, the harder and faster you push off, the more power your punch will have. Your punch should make contact about the same time that your rear foot touches the ground. In addition, a JKD practitioner gets more power if he uses a horizontal fist with the step-back punch. However, always experiment to see which fist angle works best for you.

Step-Back Straight Lead Punch

A: Because Jeremy Lynch (right) is too close to Shawn King, Lynch can't step in and execute a straight lead punch.

B: Lynch pushes off hard and fast with his front lead foot and punches King. Basically, Lynch executes a step-back punch.

C: Having moved backward, Lynch not only successfully attacks the opponent but also moves himself to a proper distance from which to launch a straight lead punch.

Push to Straight Lead Punch

A: There are other ways to get the proper distance necessary for the straight lead punch. In this case, Jeremy Lynch (right) shoves Shawn King backward with a shove-to-punch technique.

B: Lynch snaps his wrists and elbows to increase the speed and power of his shove.

C: Lynch immediately follows his push with a straight lead punch. Lynch does not have to step back because he pushes King to the proper distance.

A blast is two or more punches delivered in quick succession. As such, the JKD straight blast is another potent straight punch, which is often confused with the *wing chun* blast because both deliver fast straight punches one after another. While a stylist performing the wing chun blast squares his shoulders as he throws short, snappy punches, a jeet kune do practitioner executes his blast by throwing his shoulders and hips into two potent punches that strike one after the other. The wing chun blast has more speed, while the JKD blast has more power. In addition, Lee taught Bremer that the most effective JKD blast combination was a straight lead punch followed by a straight rear punch.

JKD Blast

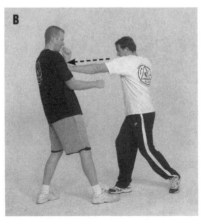

A: Jeremy Lynch (right) launches a *jeet kune do* blast at Shawn King.

B: Lynch initiates the blast from a fighting stance by throwing a short straight lead punch. The punch is short, however, because Lynch is in the brim-of-fire line.

C: Lynch doubles the potency of his attack by quickly following up with a short straight lead rear punch. Notice how the punch extends through the shoulder.

Wing Chun Blast

A: *Wing chun* blasts are shorter and snappier punches than in *jeet kune do*. They have less penetration power.

B: Jeremy Lynch (right) launches two short punches at Shawn King's chest. He could also strike the face.

Unlike in Western boxing, a JKD stylist learns that if he needs to punch an opponent more than three times, it probably means he is in trouble because the opponent is stronger than the stylist. This is why the wing chun blast, which is a series of many punches, might come in useful. By combining it with the power of a JKD hand tool, a JKD practitioner can use it in a combination blast. For example, a JKD stylist considers using a wing chun blast

Boxing Blast

A: Jeremy Lynch (right) intercepts Shawn King's straight lead punch with his left fist. He also launches a simultaneous attack while King's centerline is open.

B: Putting power behind each hook punch, Lynch throws three more consecutive blasts at his opponent's body.

C: The third blast catches King in the side.

D: The fourth punch hits King in the chin. Now, he is disabled.

to control the distance between himself and an opponent, especially if he is too close to hit his target with the desired two-inch penetration.

To attack with a JKD and wing chun blast combination, use the short straight lead punch to snap an opponent's head back to get the proper distance and then employ one or more of the straight lead punches as a finishing maneuver.

Short Wing Chun Punch and JKD Straight Lead Punch

A: Bob Bremer (right) uses a short *wing chun* punch to push back Jeremy Lynch.

B: Bremer immediately follows up his interception with a straight lead punch to the face. Because the JKD blast is a double strike, Bremer uses combinations of other punches to gain the optimum power and distance for each hit.

Short Wing Chun and JKD Punch Combination Blast

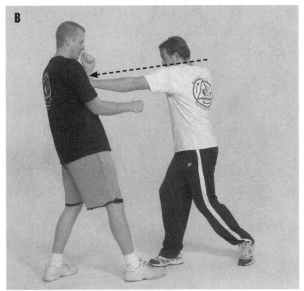

A: Jeremy Lynch starts with a quick *wing chun* punch.

B: The shorter punch sets him up for the more penetrating extension of a JKD straight lead punch.

The blasts require a great deal of power, which may become clearer if we look to Lee. In his backyard videos, Lee is striking a heavy bag with powerful hook punches. He doesn't attempt to protect himself from the swinging bag. Instead, his entire attention is focused on getting as much power as possible out of his blasts. Lee told his students that once they hurt their opponent with the first part of the blast, they should finish him off as quickly and efficiently as possible. Note: In order to make it a versatile and fluid technique, there's no concrete rule for which punches should be used in a JKD blast.

Sliding-Leverage Blast

A, B, C, D: JKD practitioners also can use blasts as a defensive technique. Note: If your opponent attempts to strike you, stop his punch with a blast that blocks his arms. Here, Shawn King (left) uses JKD blasts to defend himself against Jeremy Lynch.

Western Boxing Influence

While the straight punches listed in this chapter are sometimes confused with boxing punches, their structure is completely different. Remember, a straight lead punch is not a minor blow that sets up a fight-ending attack. Neither is it a standard wing chun punch because it uses the hip and extends through the shoulder. In the end, it is a "Bruce Lee punch" because Lee refined it. While he may have gotten his basic ideas from boxing, Lee truly made the punches his own. To make a Bruce Lee punch work, train for knockout power. If you cannot intercept with power, it's not jeet kune do. That said, the punches in this section are from Western boxing and are used in jeet kune do because Lee believed that wing chun's dominant straight lead punch limited mobility and attack angles. In addition, some of JKD's footwork and curved punch concepts come from boxing, as well.

Hook Punch

A: Shawn King (right) executes a hook punch by rotating his body and targeting the opponent's head or body. His power comes from the rotation's speed and transfer of weight from his rear to front lead foot.

B: He can also launch a low hook from a ready stance.

Hook Punch in Combination

A: A hook punch is the most efficient follow-up to a straight rear punch because of how your body is set.

B: After a straight rear punch, Shawn King (left) will be ready to twist his body into a hook, making it easier to launch.

C: In practice, King knows that a hook punch used with the straight rear punch makes proper rotation and weight transfer a necessity to get maximum punching power. Remember that the more you rotate, the more power you'll produce.

Uppercut

A: The uppercut is a close-range tool that usually targets an opponent's chin. Here, Jeremy Lynch (left) prepares to throw a hook punch. Note: Don't just lower your arm and swing because that will slow down and telegraph your attack to an opponent. Instead, lower your body (not just your punching arm) to get at the target.

B: The most efficient way to throw an uppercut is to slip inside an opponent's right straight lead punch, which provides a perfect target to the chin. From the fighting stance, Lynch steps slightly forward and to the right with his front foot in order to dodge Shawn King's punch. Lynch also rotates his body so that most of his weight is on his front foot and his left shoulder is now forward when he strikes.

Shovel Hook

A: The shovel hook is similar to the uppercut except that the punch is at a 45-degree angle and that the main target is the opponent's body.

B: The shovel hook is like scooping a heavy load on a shovel and tossing it. One of the best ways to use the shovel hook is by slipping outside an opponent's jab in the right lead stance.

C: After slipping outside an opponent's attack, punch his kidney. Notice how Jeremy Lynch transfers his weight to his front foot because the punch's power comes from pushing up with his right foot. For maximum power, Lynch angles his front foot to match the angle of his punch.

Western Boxing and JKD Combination

A, B, C: Jeremy Lynch throws a straight lead punch and then follows up his attack with a cross. After each punch, he snaps back into an on-guard (fighting) stance. Note: Cover yourself with your right hand while you punch with your left hand.

Backfists

While not very powerful, the backfist is fast and deceptive because it can be thrown from the on-guard position with very little, if any, preparation. The backfist that Lee taught Bremer differs from the ones thrown in action movies. Instead of making impact with the back of the hand, Lee believed it was better to use the knuckles because it lessens the chance of self-injury.

This makes it more difficult to aim the hand, however, which is why a JKD practitioner needs to be selective of his target. Usually, students learn to aim for the opponent's eyes, which are vulnerable and don't require power to harm. To reach the target, throw your backfist like a stationary lead punch: Penetrate two inches beyond the point of impact, use your whole body, transfer energy from the legs, etc. Remember, the move should be deceptive. Traditional martial artists usually use a lot of preparation for the strike—they cock their arm, they place their elbow at the proper angle—which gives an opponent time to react and counter it.

Classical Backfist (Front View)

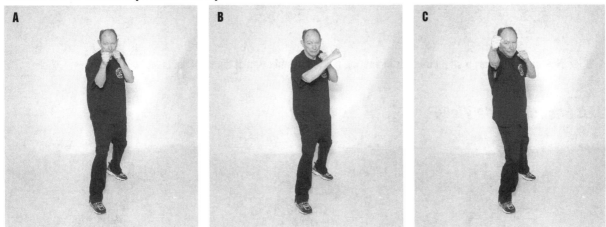

A, B, C: From the front view, notice how Tim Tackett chambers his fist before launching a backfist.

JKD Backfist (Front View)

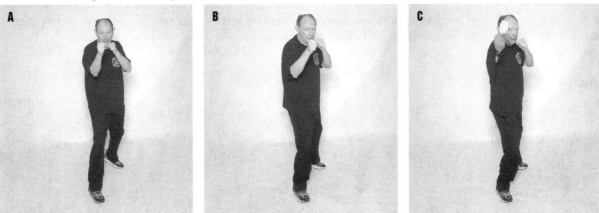

A, B, C: The JKD backfist is more deceptive than the traditional one. It looks as if Tim Tackett will launch a straight lead punch, but that is not his intention.

Classical Backfist (Side View)

A, B, C: The legs show only a slight transfer of energy, but the chambering of the right fist is obvious.

JKD Backfist (Side View)

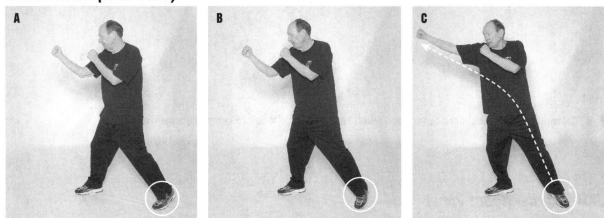

A, B, C: By twisting his rear foot to assist in energy transfer, Tim Tackett's backfist flows together as a single motion rather than two. By the time his fist reaches its target, it will be angled properly.

Backfist Blast

A: If necessary, JKD practitioners also can perform a blast with a backfist.

B: Jeremy Lynch (right) strikes first with his backfist.

C: He continues the circular motion of his body with a follow-through straight lead punch with his left hand.

Lee taught his students to throw the backfist in one motion. The classical method contains two parts: preparation and strike. However, by twisting the rear foot, Lee condensed the steps into a single move. Because all JKD strikes first appear to be straight lead punches, a JKD backfist should look like a straight lead punch at first.

Twisting the rear foot shifts the momentum, and now the attack is on its way to the target as a backfist punch. To finish a JKD backfist, flick your wrist at the last second. That's why Lee would tell his students to learn how to hurt their opponent with a flick. This idea also works with the hammerfist or backfist variations.

Other Hand Tools

Along with straight lead punches, boxing strikes and wing chun techniques, Lee had other hand tools at his disposal, including the whip principle. In fact, you've probably done it already. Have you ever flicked a towel at someone? The whip principle is that exact movement: a fast and "snappy" flick that can disable any opponent.

The same principle also applies to the "finger slice." Throw a finger slice like you would a backfist, but snap your hand back as quickly as possible into an on-guard stance. This creates a whipping motion, which flicks outward and back within the blink of an eye. Coincidentally, your main target is also the eye. This should end the fight. You truly will have done what Lee described to Bremer as "hurt[ing] with a flick"

Finger Slice

A: Tim Tackett (left) and Jeremy Lynch stand in an on-guard position.

B: Before Lynch can react, Tackett's strong lead hand slices at Lynch's eye. The finger slice should be quick and snappy. Because the eye is such a vulnerable target, the technique doesn't have to be strong to injure it.

Chapter 4
KICKING TOOLS

"Punch when you have to punch; kick when you have to kick."

—Bruce Lee, *Tao of Jeet Kune Do*

Just like hand tools, kicks need penetrative power and snap. But instead of aiming two inches beyond the point of impact, JKD practitioners aim four to six inches beyond the target when they do a thrust kick like the side kick. With less than four inches, there won't be enough force to disable an opponent. With more than six inches, a kick turns into a push.

Penetration aside, it's also important to note how a JKD practitioner initiates a kick because all jeet kune do kicking tools start the same basic way—as a front kick—until the last second. Not only does this kind of initiation allow a JKD practitioner enough mobility to shift unexpectedly into a side- or rear-kick variation, it is also deceptive because the opponent won't be able to guess what kind of kick the practitioner is launching. Basically, the opponent will be defenseless until too late.

Side Kicks and Variations

The side kick is perhaps the most adaptable of all kicks because it can be used in combination with any of the other kicking tools in this chapter. When performing a side kick, keep the factors listed in this section in mind to achieve maximum power. Also, note how the following factors might apply to other kicks:

- Kick faster to generate more power.
- Make sure the hip torques at the proper moment.
- Correctly align your body to add power.
- For greater penetration power, hit your target in the precise area that you are aiming for with your heel.
- Use the maximum amount of "snap" at the end of your kick.
- Because the side kick is a kind of thrust kick, penetrate four to six inches beyond the target.

In order to obtain the most snap, JKD practitioners train with the water-hose principle, which is similar to the elbow snap. (See Page 35.) To understand it, imagine that your leg is like a water hose. Stand with your feet parallel at about shoulder-width apart and then raise one leg. Next, drive the leg to the ground as hard as possible, locking your knee. After doing that a few times, lock your leg and quickly snap it back like you're shaking water out of a fire hose. The side kick's snapping motion should mimic how water travels through the hose.

Water-Hose Principle

A: For the first part of this exercise, Jeremy Lynch stands with his feet close to parallel and hands raised.

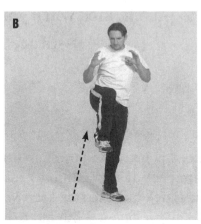

B: He raises one knee as if he is about to do a front kick, then thrusts it to the ground as hard as possible.

C: Lynch extends his leg until the joint locks.

D: He snaps back his locked leg into the chambered position like he is shaking water out of a hose.

E: The shaking motion should mimic the snap of a proper side kick.

There are two JKD side kicks: the basic side kick and the side rear kick, and both are differentiated from each other by their commitment level. ("Commitment level" means the amount of penetration or force put into a strike.) In regards to the basic side kick, it is a common tool in many martial arts, but in jeet kune do, it is less committed than other JKD kicking tools because it uses less penetration and, therefore, less power. By not extending the hip into the kick, the basic side kick is actually more suited for combination attacks and attacks based on speed. Basically, it has a quicker recovery, which means that basic side kicks are more effective in setting up attacks or defenses rather than immobilizing an opponent with one strike.

Basic Side Kick as an Attack

A: Jim Sewell and Jeremy Lynch (right) face each other from the on-guard position.

B: Lynch pivots his left foot and then thrusts out his right leg in a basic side kick.

C: Even though he penetrates his target, Lynch doesn't fully extend through his hip. Also notice how Lynch kicks with his heel and not the flat of his foot in order to avoid self-injury.

Compared to the basic side kick, the side rear kick is more powerful because it requires more commitment. By rolling and extending his hip, a JKD practitioner's kick penetrates farther and thrusts his heel beyond the impact point. However, it will take more time for him to recover his original fighting stance.

To launch an effective and damaging side rear kick, make sure that you'll hit your target. If you are certain of the distance between yourself and your opponent, throw the side rear kick.

Side Rear Kick

A: Even though this looks like the basic side kick, it isn't. Compare the stripe on Jeremy Lynch's leg in this picture and in the basic side kick sequence earlier. It is a subtle difference, but Lynch's hip rotates into the target. With the extra extension, Lynch's kick penetrates slightly farther. Because it requires more commitment, the kick delivers more power.

The slide side kick is a variation of the side kick, which allows a JKD practitioner to strike from a distance while advancing forward. To perform this kick, slide your front foot forward to close the distance between you and your opponent. Depending on how far away the target is, the rear foot either slides up a little or a lot. Rather than always moving your rear foot to where your lead foot used to be, vary how far you move your foot. By placing a line on the floor, you can practice varying the distance you slide up and launch your kick. Remember, jeet kune do is not about set attacks. To keep your opponent off-balance and unsure of your intentions, adjust the distance and rhythm of your techniques.

Slide Side Kick

A: To perform a slide side kick, start in a basic fighting stance.

B: Slide the rear foot in close so that you can maintain your balance while launching the kick.

C: Notice that the fighter's rear foot is now in the position once occupied by his front foot.

D: Once in position, extend the leg for the kick, but not as much as with a side rear kick.

Gaining More Distance With the Side Kick

A: Jeremy Lynch stands in the fighting stance.

B: He begins to transfer his weight from his rear leg to his front leg.

C: With the weight transferred, Lynch pushes his front leg forward with his rear leg.

D: Rather than a slide, the push gives him more distance.

For the same reasons given in Chapter 3 (See Page 41.), sometimes it's better to kick from an angle. In such a scenario, use a curve side kick, which is what Lee called a single angulated attack. To perform one, take a lead step out while throwing a hand feint. Follow this up by sliding your rear foot to the right and forward. Make sure to aim four to six inches beyond the target so you achieve the proper balance between penetration and power.

Curve Right Side Kick

A: Shawn King (left) and Jeremy Lynch face off at the fighting measure.

B: Lynch slides his rear foot to the right and forward to perform a curve right side kick.

C: Lynch tries to kick King while he is moving right so the attack uses the momentum of his slide.

Another variation of the side kick is the pendulum side kick, which can follow up either a hand or kick attack. It is also a good example of what Lee might have meant in regards to the idea of, "punch when you have to punch [and kick] when you have to kick." While this sounds like simple advice, most people learn to follow up a kick with a kick and a punch with a punch. During a real fight, however, you'll need to use combinations with both, and the pendulum side kick is a good transition move to use between techniques. That's why in training, you should spar with your partner in such as way that you need to kick, punch, retreat, come in close and use different openings to attack.

Pendulum Kick

A: In a fighting stance, Jeremy Lynch slides forward and then swings his leg straight up like a pendulum.

B: He brings his kicking leg up as fast as possible so he can quickly follow up with another attack.

C: Back at his original position, Lynch is now at a distance where he can launch any attack.

While the previous side kicks work at both long and midrange, JKD practitioners also throw side kicks at close range. Two examples are the downward side kick and stomp kick. The downward side kick works at close range because it travels up from the floor, and the stomp kick works because it targets an opponent's foot.

Also note, that these two kicks still work from the fighting measure. If your opponent moves closer when you initiate a side kick, you can easily switch it to a downward side kick or stomp kick. However, the stomp kick is usually more effective at an even closer range as compared to the downward side kick

Downward Side Kick

A: Shawn King and Jeremy Lynch (right) face each other in the fighting measure. They are farther away than they actually would be in a real fighting situation.

B: Lynch launches a downward side kick at his opponent.

C: Because Lynch targets the knee, King can't intercept the attack with his foot or hands.

Stomp Kick

A: Even though Shawn King and Jeremy Lynch (right) start in the fighting measure, Lynch closes the distance during the attack.

B: Lynch looks like he is launching a front kick rather than a side kick, making the move more deceptive.

C: Lynch strikes the foot.

Another close-range kick is the JKD groin kick, which is a simple strike to perform. To do it properly, lift your leg up with enough of an angle to clear your opponent's knee and then snap your leg toward his groin. Because it is so simple, there is little or no preparation, which adds to its deceptiveness. Remember, your power comes from lifting your leg and throwing the kick from your hip.

JKD Groin Kick

A: The JKD groin kick is easy to do when you are close to your opponent.

B: Like all other side kicks, the groin kick starts out as a front kick. Shawn King (right) will think that Jeremy Lynch plans to kick high.

C: Pivoting on his rear foot, Lynch's foot finds its target.

The oblique kick is another close-range kick and can be performed with either the front or rear leg, although the rear leg works best. With the rear leg, the kick will be more powerful because it has to travel farther to reach its target. Because it is a close-range kick that

Oblique Kick

A: From a fighting stance, Jeremy Lynch (right) thrusts his rear leg straight up and kicks Shawn King's knee.

B: Because balance is so important for this move, practice recovering a lot. After the technique, Lynch must prepare to recover for his next attack.

is usually thrown from a stationary stance, the kick should go straight from the floor to the target. Often, the target is the knee.

While not as well-known, the butterfly kick is also an effective close-range tool. It is a combination kick that uses the oblique kick followed by a JKD groin kick. The technique gets its characteristic name from the combined movement of the two side kicks.

Butterfly Kick

A: To do the butterfly kick, use the oblique kick first to distract the opponent's attention.

B: Then throw the groin kick while retracting the oblique kick. Don't return to your fighting stance until you have launched both kicks in rapid succession.

Remember, no matter which side kick a JKD stylist throws, there is no way to move forward without an opponent seeing it. In addition, the stylist's choice in target greatly affects the successful outcome of his kick. For example, if he tries to target his opponent's midsection from a distance, he'll most likely overextend his kick and fall off-balance because his opponent will retreat.

To help deceive your opponent, keep your kick low and use your hand as a distraction. Throwing a feint with your lead hand distracts an opponent from seeing your kick and intention, but remember to keep your hand feint in place for the duration of the move. One of the best ways to practice this is by taking a lead step with your hand feint and then following it with a slide and kick.

Hand Feint With a Slide and Kick

A: Jeremy Lynch prepares to do a slide and kick. The stick on the ground shows how he will advance forward through his feint.

B: Taking a lead step forward, Lynch feints high with his hand. Imagine that his hand is inches from his opponent's face.

C: With a quick slide, Lynch launches into the air but keeps his hand in place.

D: When he lands, he immediately strikes with a side kick.

Front Kicks and Variations

Front kicks are also an option in jeet kune do, but they are not as prevalent as side kicks because they are less deceptive. However, here are two options for front kicks:

The scoop kick is an easy front kick to perform at all three ranges because it can be thrown with a bent knee when a JKD practitioner is close to his opponent. He can also kick with a straighter knee when he is farther away. As a straight kick, the scoop kick uses the whip principle instead of the water-hose principle to snap the knee and ankle for power and speed. Because it is an angular kick rather than a thrust kick, the scoop kick combined with the whip principle will only penetrate one inch to three inches depending on the target.

Basic Scoop Kick

A, B, C: When at long range, simply slide up to your opponent, lift your knee and snap a kick into the opponent's groin.

Scoop Kick at Close Range

A, B: At close range, grab onto your opponent to balance yourself and keep him in place while you perform the scoop kick.

Scoop Kick at Long Range

A, B, C: Jeremy Lynch (left) uses a hand feint to distract Shawn King while he moves in closer. Once he's close enough, Lynch launches a scoop kick.

The front thrust kick is a potent front stop-kick for intercepting a hand attack from the natural stance. Unlike other JKD kicks, this technique must be chambered to get power. This is one of the few exceptions to the rule because a JKD practitioner must have the right angle to hit the target. It also uses the water-hose principle.

Front Thrust Kick

A: Shawn King (left) approaches Jeremy Lynch, who is in the natural stance. (See Page 10.)

B: To avoid telegraphing his move, Lynch chambers as he kicks and not before.

C: Lynch thrusts his leg outward as if he was putting on a pair of pants.

Hook Kicks and Variations

Borrowing principles from boxing, Lee incorporated the roundhouse kick into jeet kune do and called it the "hook kick." He chose to maintain the term "hook" because it follows the same line as a boxer's hook punch. (See Page 50.) However, like other JKD kicking tools, the hook kick is deceptive because it requires very little chambering. It also should look like a front kick until the last second.

The hook kick gets its power from the rotation of the body and hips, as well as the speed and snap of the leg by using the whip principle. At the last second after initiation, rotate your body and hips just like a person hitting a baseball with a bat. Make sure that your knee penetrates at least two to four inches before you recover so that your kick goes through the impact point. Also, snap your leg back as fast or faster than you send it to the target. You will make contact with the toe, instep or shin depending on what type of shoes you are wearing. (Note: Because people spend most of the day wearing shoes, it only makes sense for JKD practitioners to train in shoes instead of barefoot. There is no special JKD workout gear.)

Basic Hook Kick

A: Jeremy Lynch (left) throws a high hand feint before he launches a lower kick because it will distract his opponent.

B: Lynch's knee must travel at least three to four inches past his target. This technique can be used to target any vulnerable part of the body.

In the unmatched stance, a JKD practitioner can target his opponent's groin with an inverted hook kick. To throw one, slide up to the opponent as you raise your front foot past his groin. Then, snap your leg toward the target—which in this case is the groin—to immobilize your adversary.

Inverted Hook Kick

A: Jeremy Lynch (right) throws a hand feint to distract his opponent.

B: Like with the hook kick, Lynch's knee should travel past the target, without knocking him off-balance. Note: Make sure to rotate your knee and hip toward the target at the last second.

Another variation of the hook kick is the heel hook kick, which is often misrepresented in movies. High heel kicks are impressive, but they leave a JKD stylist's Achilles tendon and calf vulnerable to serious injury. However, when thrown low, this kick is an effective sweeping technique that JKD stylists can execute with either a bent or straight leg.

Straight Heel Hook Kick

A, B, C: From the unmatched stance, Jeremy Lynch (right) slides up to his opponent while swinging his front heel toward the inside of Shawn King's knee.

Bent Leg Heel Hook Kick

A, B: This is performed the same way as the straight heel hook kick, but the knee is bent. Note: Whether you use a straight or bent knee is up to you.

Crescent Kicks

There are two kinds of crescent kicks: the inward crescent kick and the outward crescent kick. While these kicks may not seem very powerful, proficient fighters like Lee use them as potent attacks because they use the speed and weight of the leg to gain penetration power. For example, Lee once gave Bremer a focus glove to hold and landed such a powerful crescent

Inward Crescent Kick

A: All crescent kicks are circular straight-legged kicks that can be performed with either the front or rear leg.

B: Slide up with a straight leg. Notice that it looks like a front kick.

C: Throw your right leg counterclockwise into your opponent's hand or head.

kick on his arm that Bremer was sore for a week. However, remember that crescent kicks require strong commitment, which is why it is safer and more efficient for JKD practitioners, as even demonstrated by Lee, to use these kicks to target an opponent's lead hand.

Outward Crescent Kick

A: Start this kick by sliding up as you raise your rear straight foot.

B: Swing it counterclockwise into your opponent's hand or head.

Training

We've discussed how kicks should begin, but also remember that recovery is just as important in an attack. A JKD stylist doesn't want to launch a kick, hit his target and then fail to properly return to an on-guard position because he a) lost his balance, b) took a wrong step or c) was countered by his opponent. To avoid this danger, practice returning to your stance, along with developing enough penetration power to still execute an effective attack. For example, in the Wednesday Night Group, students use kick shields to train for kicking and recovering. If a student launches a kick at a kick shield but fails to recover decently, his partner, who is holding the shield, charges and pushes him off-balance.

Part II
Advanced Principles

A Note to Readers

This section covers attacks, defenses, JKD principles and specialized tools like the hammer principle and leg obstruction. Because some of these tools are seldom taught, readers should approach this section with a solid understanding of the basic techniques discussed in Part I. If you find that certain techniques don't work for you or are too hard, then by all means, do what is best for you. Remember what Lee wrote in *Tao of Jeet Kune Do*: "A jeet kune do man faces [the] reality and not crystallization of form. The tool is a tool of formless form." The glossary is also available to help readers who are unfamiliar with common JKD terms.

Chapter 5
DEFENSES

"It is a correct maxim that a good offense is the best defense."

—Bruce Lee, *Tao of Jeet Kune Do*

Martial artists in the 1960s often considered defense as a block followed by a counter-attack. However, despite the concept's roots in traditional arts, this type of defense has an inherent problem: a time lag. No matter how skilled the martial artist, he can't respond instantaneously to an attack, especially if he blocks it. A slight delay always exists between a block and follow-up attack, and this creates the perfect opportunity for a creative opponent to use to his advantage.

That doesn't mean that JKD practitioners never use the block and hit; rather, they just understand that it's not the most effective way to stop an opponent. Nor is the basic wing chun defense—a simultaneous block-hit—the most effective. Instead, a JKD practitioner knows that the answer to the most potent defense lies in Lee's studies on Western fencing. In a duel, a fencer tries to intercept and deflect an attack with his own attack; this is called a "stop-hit." Lee found that the stop-hit is more potent than either the block and hit or simultaneous block-hit because it involves fewer movements, is quicker to execute and is, in essence, an attack. Basically, the ideal JKD scenario involves a stop-hit because the JKD stylist defends himself by beating his opponent to the punch.

Block and Hit

A: The best way to help students under-
stand defense time lags is to show them.
Here, Jeremy Lynch (left) faces off with
Shawn King.

B: King throws a loose hook by stepping into the brim-of-fire line, but Lynch
blocks the strike.

C: After Lynch blocks the strike, there's
a slight delay before Lynch can deliver a
straight lead punch.

Simultaneous Block and Hit

A: In this sequence, Jeremy Lynch (left) simultaneously
intercepts and strikes Shawn King.

B: When King throws a high hook, Lynch steps in with an
inside parry and a straight lead punch. He condenses his
defense into a smaller amount of time, which denies his
adversary any openings.

However, no matter which method of countering a JKD practitioner uses—stop-hit, block
and hit, or simultaneous block-hit—the key to JKD defense is interception because it is a
strike that is a means to a) avoid being hit and b) stop an opponent's attack before it reaches
the practitioner. In jeet kune do, the ideal interception is with a stop-hit or simultaneous

block-hit because they rely more on the power of a strike than that of a block for defense. Basically, they are not passive moves because the JKD practitioner is always on the offense, even in his defense.

To properly intercept an attack, a JKD practitioner must perceive his opponent's intentions. Fencers call this type of perception "attack on preparation," which refers to how a fighter can read and intercept an opponent's attack even before he does it through a tense shoulder or eye movement. There is also "attack on delivery," which refers to how a fighter reads and intercepts an opponent's attack just as it starts but before it reaches its target. Of course, the difficulty with attack on preparation is that a JKD practitioner must be extremely quick and intuitive of his opponent's movements, and this takes practice. In regards to attacking on delivery, a JKD stylist is in trouble if he's not fast and quick enough to take advantage of that split-second opening; he might miss the chance to launch a defense at all. But however he reads an oncoming attack, the JKD practitioner needs to recognize what hand or kicking tool his opponent is using, decide on a method to avoid it through interception, and then launch his stop-hit quickly and effectively.

Stop-Hits

For JKD practitioners, stop-hits are the most successful way to intercept an attack. Rather than complicating the move with two hands or a block, a stop-hit is a one-handed attack whose sole purpose is to hit an opponent before his strike hits its target. This makes stop-hits effective against an opponent who is a) preparing for an attack, b) feinting or faking an attack or c) using wide attacking motions like swinging his fist. Because many martial arts teach blocking as the first line of defense, a clever opponent might use a block to switch to an open line to prepare for a more potent attack through a fake. With a stop-hit, the opponent has no choices. He can't fake out or feint the JKD practitioner because no matter what he does, the practitioner's first line of defense is to hit rather than block his strike. In the matter of a wide swing, the stop-hit takes advantage of the time lag and simply beats the opponent to the punch.

In order to do a successful stop-hit, a JKD practitioner needs a lot of training, agility and a strong intuitive ability to sense an attack on preparation. He also needs to control the fighting measure with footwork because a successful counterattack depends on proper distance. If he's in close range, the JKD practitioner takes the chance of reading an opponent's intentions too late and won't have time to respond to the attack. If he's beyond the fighting measure, the JKD practitioner narrows his list of potential targets. In addition to maintaining proper distance and speed, the JKD stylist also must know when to perform a stop-hit properly during a fight:

- Attack on preparation, which is anytime before the attack is launched. For example, a JKD stylist may see the opponent take a step forward, which may signal his intent to launch a straight lead punch that must be intercepted.
- Attack on delivery, which is in the middle of an opponent's attacking motion, just after

it starts but before it hits its target. The force of a JKD practitioner's stop-hit increases because the adversary is moving into the strike.

- Attack on completion, which is when the opponent's attack reaches full extension because the opponent will be open both inside and under his punching arm.
- Attack on recovery, which is just before the opponent recovers his original fighting stance after his attack because he will be open on the inside or outside of his punching arm, or he may even be open on a straight line to his head, but only if he drops his arm.

Attack on Preparation

A: At the fighting measure, Jeremy Lynch (right) tries to sense whether his opponent is preparing for an attack. He looks for any clues that will help him read Shawn King's intentions, like a tense muscle.

B: King retracts his hand in preparation for a punch. Notice how Lynch transfers his energy forward immediately to launch a straight lead punch.

C: King is never given the opportunity to step forward or bring his attack past its preparation point. Lynch's strong lead hand and push-step guarantee that he connects with his opponent in a miniscule amount of time.

Attack on Delivery

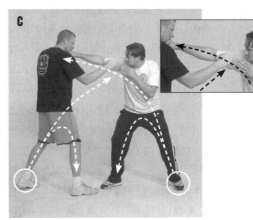

A: To intercept an attack on delivery, a JKD practitioner wants to hit an opponent before the opponent hits him.

B: Shawn King (left) and Jeremy Lynch have launched punches. Lynch, however, is defending himself against King's strike with a stop-hit, which means he must be quicker.

C: Lynch succeeds with his stop-hit. Notice how he extends his right arm for impact but also slips slightly to the outside to avoid being hit.

Another way to consider when to use a stop-hit is by hitting on or between the beat. When an opponent strikes, he creates an opening and a closing line of attack. The opening line of attack is the line drawn from the beginning of the strike to full extension, while the closing line is the line drawn from full extension to recovery. The full beat is at the exact midpoint between the opening and closing lines on the focal point, or when the arm is fully extended (attack on completion). The half beat is located between the start of the opening line and the

Hitting on the Half Beat (Attack on Delivery)

A: Jeremy Lynch (left) and Tim Tackett stand in matching fighting stances.

B: When Lynch's strike hits the half beat, Tackett launches a stop-hit.

C: Because his hit is faster than Lynch's, Tackett lands his hit first.

Hitting on the Full Beat (Attack on Completion)

A: Tim Tackett (left) and Jeremy Lynch are in matching fighting stances.

B: When Lynch's strike extends, Tackett punches back. Because he moves so quickly and blocks with his left hand, Tackett beats Lynch to the punch.

focal point (attack on delivery). The one-and-a-half beat occurs as the closing line begins, or the strike is fully extended, and then retracts back to its original position (attack on recovery). In jeet kune do, a practitioner tries whenever possible to intercept an opponent's attack on the half beat because it stops the strike cold. Because the opponent is stopped before he can complete his attack, he'll also have no way to counter the JKD practitioner's strike. Remember that timing is of the essence and practice is just as vital because it's not easy to read an opponent's attack and beat him with enough power to end a fight.

It's also possible to hit during the time lag between two motions of a combination attack, but also remember that in addition to awareness, speed, footwork and penetration power (with the strong hand forward) add to the potency of a stop-hit. Of course, making all these elements work together takes a lot of practice, which is why so much of JKD training focuses on practicing stop-hits against various attacks. In addition, remember to practice all your defensive stop-hits from both fighting stances and the natural stance in order to figure out how each will work best for you in a fight.

Protecting the Four Corners

Whether a JKD practitioner does a stop-hit or another form of interception, he still needs to protect his body, which means he must defend the "four corners." As a concept that Lee originally learned in wing chun, the four corners are as follows:

• The high inside gate, which is the area inside the lead arm and above the elbow.
• The high outside gate, which is the area outside the lead arm and above the elbow.
• The low inside gate, which is the area inside the lead arm and below the elbow.
• The low outside gate, which is the area outside the lead arm and below the elbow.

Four Corners

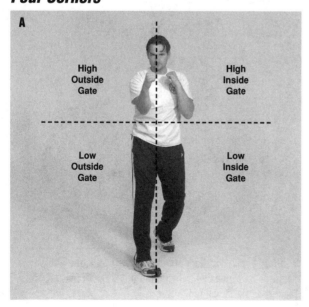

A: To defend the four corners, a JKD practitioner stands in one of the fighting stances with his hands in the proper position, covering the centerline. Bruce Lee also thought it is just as important to practice four-corner defense against a matching stance and unmatched stance in order to maintain optimum mobility.

In wing chun, martial artists defend the four corners mostly through straight punches, which Lee believed was too limiting, especially after his San Francisco Chinatown challenge. (See Introduction.) He modified the concepts with his knowledge of Western boxing defense so that he could deal with curved and angulated movements. Lee's modification also guaranteed that JKD practitioners can more easily "attack on intention" if they defend the four corners. Because the JKD fighting stances effectively cover a defender's centerline (from the top of your head to your groin) an opponent has no choice but to attack with a curved or angulated strike. This then helps the JKD practitioner pick up the opponent's intent and know how to combine his straight defense with a mobile and angulated interception.

However, the best four-corner defense against an angulated attack is still a stop-hit because it is fast and lacks clicks. A "click" is a term Lee used to illustrate speed and fluidity to his students. By looking at a filmstrip of a technique, Lee demonstrated how that continuous technique was in reality a series of still photographs; he called each photo a click. Lee said that one of the main objectives of jeet kune do is to eradicate these clicks, which is why the stop-hit is preferred to a block and hit or simultaneous block-hit.

Proper Click Count

A, B, C: The stop-hit against a high hook punch, followed by a block, condenses the number of clicks by one. Even this small difference increases the defense's speed and makes it more difficult for Shawn King (right) to counterattack or pick up on Jeremy Lynch's intent.

Improper Click Count

A, B, C, D: Four clicks make up this block and hit against a high hook punch, which is demonstrated by Tim Tackett (left) and Jeremy Lynch. Remember that Bruce Lee viewed blocking as a passive form of defense that isn't very effective.

The sliding-leverage principle also helps JKD practitioners reduce the number of clicks in a technique, thus, helping to defend the four corners. Instead of intercepting an attack straight on, the JKD practitioner "cuts into" a strike by sliding to the side, meaning he moves to an open line and intercepts. This maintains his fluidity of motion. For example, consider two opponents who face each other in unmatched fighting stances. The attacker strikes on the inside line, meaning he punches inside the defender's front arm (high inside gate). The defender can cut into his adversary's tool by sliding off the line of attack and intercepting from an angle. If attacked from an outside line, meaning the attacker punches outside the front arm (high outside gate), the defender can slide inside the line of attack and intercept from an angle.

Sliding Leverage in Action Against an Inside Line of Attack

A: Tim Tackett (right) faces Jeremy Lynch in a matching fighting stance.

B: Lynch launches a straight lead punch on the inside line, but Tackett slides to an open line on the right of his opponent's punching arm.

C: He cuts into Lynch's tool by launching an angulated attack that makes contact with his nose or eye. Tackett keeps his elbow slightly bent until he makes contact, maintaining the angle of his interception. He also properly transfers his weight through his front leg as well as rotates his body for optimum power.

Sliding Leverage in Action Against an Outside Line of Attack

A: Tim Tackett (right) faces Jeremy Lynch in an unmatched fighting stance.

B: Lynch launches a strike to the outside (high outside gate) line, but Tackett is prepared. He cuts into the hand tool by squaring his shoulders and shooting a right finger jab directly to the adversary's eye. Because the hit is horizontal, the twist of the elbow forces Tackett's aim to an open line.

C: While Tackett could also defend himself without a block in this scenario, it's safer that he uses one. He just needs to make sure his success doesn't depend on it.

Sliding Leverage in Action Against a Left Hook

A: Tim Tackett (right) stands against Jeremy Lynch in an unmatched stance.

B: Lynch throws a left hook at Tackett's head. Tackett cuts into the tool by throwing a vertical hook to Lynch's jaw.

C: Tackett also tucks his head behind his shoulder and covers the side of his face with his hand as a safety factor. Because the movement will disrupt Lynch's strike, it will also slide Tackett to an open line, making the defense fluid and fast.

Blocking

Even though Lee thought blocking was the least efficient method of defense, he still recognized its value in a fight, especially when a JKD stylist is ambushed or unprepared for an attack. Many of the blocks used in jeet kune do come from Western boxing and are taught as a defense against Western boxing hand tools. JKD instructors also tend to use blocks as an effective teaching method for students. Because they involve a time lag, they are easier for a beginner to learn and are safer to use when a student begins contact training. However, blocks change into interceptions, especially when the student becomes more comfortable and capable with the techniques.

As assimilated from Western boxing, the "catch" and "cuff" are commonly useful as blocking techniques in jeet kune do. The catch is a good block because it stops the punch without opening up a JKD practitioner's centerline. In contrast, the cuff is an old boxing technique that is rarely taught anymore. However, it's good to know because it is a useful tool for anyone who wants to block a punch and then shoot for the leg, which is generally an unexpected combination and more deceptive. Also, remember that blocks are done separately or simultaneously with a hit; it just depends on how prepared a JKD practitioner is for an attack.

Catch and Hit

A: The catch is performed from a stationary position or by taking a slight step back with the rear foot. Jeremy Lynch (left) will perform the block in this sequence.

B: Lynch catches Shawn King's punch in his hand the same way he would catch a hard-thrown baseball. Depending on how hard the punch is, Lynch can either a) stay and catch the punch, b) take a slight step back by push-stepping backward or c) just take a small step back with his rear leg.

C: After catching the right jab, Lynch counters with a straight lead punch while he maintains his hold on King's right fist.

Catch With a Simultaneous Hit

A: To attack on completion means that Jeremy Lynch (right) needs to intercept Jim Sewell's strike when it is at full extension or at the focal point.

B: By transferring his weight to his front leg as he catches, Lynch ends up avoiding a direct hit to his face. It also allows him the rotation necessary to fully extend his arm for a stop-hit straight lead punch. Notice how a simultaneous hit with a catch contains less clicks.

The Cuff

A: The cuff is an upward catch that lets a JKD practitioner move in close to strike at his opponent's body. This also allows grapplers to take their opponent to the ground with more ease.

B: Jeremy Lynch (left) "pops" Shawn King's punch upward with a cuff. Because King is distracted by the block, Lynch can easily move in closer.

C: Lynch goes in for a single-leg take-down that is common in grappling. He's able to do this because he's pushed his opponent's fist upward and can duck under the punch.

Catch With a Heel and Toe Sway (Attack on Recovery)

A: When Jeremy Lynch (left) strikes with a straight lead punch, Tim Tackett catches the hit. When Tackett does this, he quickly drops his weight back to his rear foot by dropping his heel to the ground, which creates a subtle swaying motion. This is all done on the full beat.

B: Tackett then quickly transfers his weight back to his front foot as he launches an intercepting hit, which will hit Lynch at the one-and-a-half beat during his recovery.

The catch is also an effective defense to use against an attack on recovery. Like an attack on preparation or delivery, attack on recovery is a fencing term that Lee used to describe an interception that is made when an opponent returns his striking limb to its starting point in the fighting stance. An attack on recovery is also called a "response hit" because it is just that: a response to an attack. In the case of a catch, a JKD practitioner can use the block as a platform from which to launch an interception when the opponent attempts to recover.

Evasions

Another method of defense is avoiding the punch all together through evasion. There are many different ways to evade a punch by a) avoiding the strike all together, b) moving inside or outside to an open line in order to counterattack, c) angling inside or outside the strike or d) moving away from the attack. By doing any of these evasions, a JKD practitioner gives himself more time to assess the situation and decide on the proper course of action.

One specific evasion technique is the "slip," which a JKD practitioner uses to move to the outside or inside of an oncoming punch from a matching or unmatched stance. Note that when in the right lead matching stance, the practitioner pays attention to whether his opponent's elbow is too far out because it signals the adversary's intent; his punch is heading for the right side of the JKD practitioner's head. This makes it easier for the practitioner to slip outside the punch because he knows that his opponent's fist is aiming for the farthest inside corner of his face.

To slip properly in either stance from a left lead, take a step forward a few inches and to the left with your front foot; this gives the opponent's punch enough room to clear your head. Make sure you don't step forward too much because you want your punch to land a split second before your foot touches the ground. Try to punch as you move, not after. You can also do an outside block with your rear hand as a safety factor.

Slip and Counter From the Matching Stance

A: Jeremy Lynch (left) and Shawn King face off in matching stances. King will throw a straight rear punch, which means that Lynch can elect to slip outside his punch and then hit him with a high or low counter.

B: Notice how both fighters have launched punches. This means Lynch had either thought that his opponent would attack on preparation or delivery and reacted accordingly.

C: Because he successfully slips past the punch to an outside line, Lynch finishes his own finger-jab strike to King's eye.

Slip and Counter From an Unmatched Stance

A: Jeremy Lynch (left) and Shawn King are in unmatched stances.

B: King attacks with a straight left lead punch, which Lynch slips past. To help him do this, Lynch uses an outside block with his right hand.

C: Once he slips past King, Lynch counterattacks with a punch to the head or body with his left hand.

Whether in the unmatched or matching stance, a JKD practitioner calculates when and how to slip a punch by considering various factors that include stance. His decision also depends on where he is in relation to his opponent, to his intended target, on the choice of his counterattack or as to his personal preference, meaning the practitioner may feel more natural slipping to the inside than the outside line. However, a JKD practitioner may find that it's easier and safer to slip to the outside of a straight lead punch when in the unmatched stance. This is because, after a JKD stylist slips to the outside, it is difficult for an opponent to use his rear hand to defend himself.

Slip and Counter to the Inside Line From the Matching Stance

A: Jeremy Lynch (left) and Shawn King face off in matching stances.

B: When King strikes with a straight lead punch, Lynch slips to the inside line.

C: As Lynch evades, he also throws a high cross across King's punching arm to hit his head. As a safety measure, he covers his adversary's rear hand with his front hand.

Another form of evasion is the "curved right," which a JKD practitioner performs any time his opponent throws a straight lead or curved punch from a matching stance. To do it, step out and to the right, leading with your lead foot, and punch. Then, slide your rear foot so you are back in the fighting stance with your front foot between the opponent's two feet. Now, your opponent has no base and his groin is vulnerable.

If the attack isn't fluid, your groin will be vulnerable, too. In photographs, the curved right looks like three separate movements: a punch, a step with the front foot and then a step with the rear foot. This leaves a JKD practitioner open to an attack. Instead, think of the movements as 1A, 1B and 1C so the steps flow together. If your timing is right, your punch will land slightly before your front foot touches the ground, making this technique a defensive *and* offensive maneuver.

Correct Curved Right

A: Tim Tackett (left) and Jeremy Lynch face off in matching stances.

B: When Lynch launches his lead strike, Tackett simultaneously steps to the side and throws a curved punch that lands slightly before he completes the side step.

C: Tackett not only evades his opponent's attack but also launches his own successful strike. Because Tackett flows quickly from movement to movement, there is no chance for Lynch to strike his groin.

Incorrect Curved Right

A, B, C: Because Tim Tackett (right) performs each motion separately, he leaves himself open and Jeremy Lynch can easily target his groin.

Curved Right From an Unmatched Stance

A: In the unmatched stance, Jeremy Lynch (left) can only defend one side of his body, despite having a strong base. This makes Tim Tackett's intended curved right harder for him to slip past.

B: Tackett steps forward and right, throwing a curved punch just like he did in the matching stance. He also angles away from Jeremy Lynch's lead leg and striking arm, making sure Lynch can't use them to his advantage.

Steps, such as the "quick-step," are also simple, versatile and effective evasions. Favored by Ted Wong—Lee's last private student—the quick-step moves the JKD practitioner to an open line of attack where it is easy to launch an attack but difficult for the opponent to counter.

From a right lead, take a solid step left and forward by a few inches. To return to your original fighting stance, quickly follow the lead foot with a solid step from your rear foot. "Quick" is the keyword here because the step requires you to cross your feet, leaving you

Quick-Step

A: In the unmatched stance, Tim Tackett (right) defends himself against Jeremy Lynch.

B: With his lead right foot, Tackett steps to the left while simultaneously blocking a left jab.

C: Because he's stepped into an open line, Tackett launches a straight lead punch with his right hand. Not only is his centerline safe from attack, Lynch also can't do anything to counterattack.

vulnerable; but this is why you must perform the move fast enough to keep your opponent from gaining any advantage. Finally, simultaneously strike the opponent's head while quick-stepping.

It's also just as easy to "step-out" or away from an opponent to evade a strike. In the quick-step, a JKD practitioner crosses his legs in a forward diagonal direction. The step-out differs from the quick-step because it is more mobile. With this evasion, the practitioner can step out, forward, backward or to the side and attack with the lead or rear foot; it depends on what direction he wants to go. The step-out also allows the JKD practitioner to use a hand

Step-Out With a Kicking Tool

A: Shawn King (left) and Jeremy Lynch face off in unmatched stances.

B: When King launches a left lead jab, Lynch steps out with his rear foot. This makes the move more deceptive because King will most likely pay closer attention to Lynch's lead hand and foot.

C: Now Lynch is able to counterattack with an inverted kick to the groin because he is in an open line.

Step-Out With a Hand Tool

A: Tim Tackett (right) stands in the unmatched stance against Jeremy Lynch.

B: Tackett steps out to the left to evade Lynch's punch.

C: When he is on an open line, Tackett throws a straight lead punch at Lynch's face. Notice how Tackett began evading during Lynch's delivery, which assures that his own counterattack hits when Lynch's arm is extended to the focal point.

or kicking tool, depending on which line is open to attack.

Note: No matter what evasion or block he performs, an opponent is always at least one-third open whenever a JKD practitioner moves to a better offensive position.

Step-Out and Proper Distance

A: Step-outs not only move JKD practitioners to open lines of attack but also give them the proper distance to launch their defense.

B: When Shawn King (left) strikes, Jeremy Lynch steps out but slightly backward to gain proper kicking distance.

C: When his evasion is complete, he performs a hook kick to the groin or knee. Because King's strike is at the focal point, he can't defend himself with a counter.

The Beat

A: Facing Shawn King, Jeremy Lynch (right) stands in a matching stance.

B: When King steps forward with a jab, Lynch steps out with his rear foot and backward to evade the punch. However, he keeps his lead hand in front of him to measure the beat. As soon as King's striking arm comes in contact with Lynch's lead hand, he knows the beat is hit, meaning Lynch is close enough to attack but far enough to avoid a counterattack. When the beat is hit, Lynch launches a kick to the groin.

When stepping out in a backward direction, "the beat" is a useful distance gauge. Don't confuse this beat with the beats mentioned earlier in the chapter (See Page 81.); the two are separate concepts and only share the same name. Instead, this beat lets a JKD stylist know that he is outside his opponent's striking range but is still close enough to land a kick.

Defense Against Kicking Tools

If you have ever tried to block a strong, fast Thai-boxing roundhouse, you have probably learned that blocking a kick is a bad idea. This leaves four basic ways to deal with a leg attack by a) moving into the kick and intercepting it, b) jamming it up, c) avoiding the kick by angling away from it or d) staying outside its range.

To intercept a kick, the stop-kick is the way to go. However, doing so requires both the confidence and ability to move quickly into an attack. As soon as you "feel" or see a kick coming, push-step forward as fast and as hard as you can to hit your target. While almost any kick is useful to stop your opponent in his tracks, the best counter is a side kick to the opponent's knee or shin. By doing this, the only way your opponent can touch you with any hand attack is to step toward you and into the brim-of-fire line. This means that before his attack is halfway through, you can stop-kick him and then check his counterattack.

Proper Stop-Kick

A: Two opponents stand in the matching stance. Jeremy Lynch (right) perceives that Shawn King is about to throw a kick.

B: The front stop-kick to the knee begins as a straight slide step forward from the rear foot. The front foot, however, is the one that makes contact. As King starts to punch, Lynch slides up with his rear leg for interception with a kicking tool.

C: The side stop-kick to King's knee helps Lynch maintain the fighting measure. Notice how King can't reach him with a hand or leg tool.

Improper Stop-Kick

A: Remember, counterattacks can happen even though an intercepting strike, like the stop-kick, is supposed to prevent them.

B: That's why it's important for a JKD practitioner to keep his hands up when performing a stop-kick. Picture B depicts a proper stop-kick; Jeremy Lynch's hands are up.

C: In this scenario, Lynch (right) fails to properly protect his centerline and is hit by Shawn King.

Stop-Kick Against a Rear Kick

A: Shawn King (left) launches a spinning hook kick against Jeremy Lynch.

B: From the moment the kick begins to the moment when it should make contact, there will be a time lag during which King won't be looking at Lynch.

C: As he turns to look at his target, it's already too late: Lynch stops him with a front thrust kick.

One of the best ways to deal with a kick is "the jam," even though it is a seldom-taught tool. To jam, slide forward far enough to slam the side of your body and hip into your opponent's midsection. Also, raise your bent leg while sliding forward. When done with the proper timing and distance, this will smother an opponent's kick. Basically, you need to throw yourself into your opponent to make the jam work. The footwork is the same as a stop-kick, but you need

Side Stop-Kick Against a Side Kick

A: Shawn King (left) and Jeremy Lynch face each other in unmatched stances.

B: When King launches a side kick, Lynch—because of his ability to read King's preparation or delivery—launches a stop-kick.

C: Striking the back of the knee, Lynch effectively stops the attack, unbalances King and maintains the fighting measure.

Jam Against a Front-Leg Hook Kick

A: In the matching stance, Jeremy Lynch (right) and Shawn King face off.

B: Lynch jams King's hook kick by sliding forward and lifting his front bent knee. By slamming his body forward and into the kicking tool, Lynch effectively intercepts the strike.

to penetrate much deeper because your whole body is "stopping" your opponent. Performing the move successfully requires a lot of practice and a superb sense of timing. Most of the time, you will end up "jamming" with the side of your leg.

Jam Against a Rear-Leg Hook Kick

A: Even if Shawn King (left) strikes with his rear leg, Jeremy Lynch can jam him up.

B: Notice how Lynch keeps his rear arm up to block and his lead hand ready to follow up with a punch.

Angling away from a kick means moving away from the attack's force. This maneuver not only negates some of the force of an adversary's strike but also gives a JKD practitioner time to counterattack. To use angling as a defense, move away from the kick at the right time. If you move too early, your opponent can alter his attack to follow you as you angle. If you

Angle to the Right

A: Because angling is such a slight and deceptive evasion, it is difficult to see even in pictures. In this case, Shawn King (right) will perform the defense and interception.

B: Notice how King moves to an open line that is not directly in front of his opponent. This is the correct angle—a subtle 45-degree angle away from the direction of the opponent's incoming hook kick. Think of it as footwork, like the side step, but at an angle. Remember, in order to attack on intention, the fighter must have a finely honed intuitive ability.

C: From this point, Jeremy Lynch is unaware that his attack won't make contact with penetrating power because his target, King's body, is angled away. This leaves Lynch's centerline open and gives King a chance to launch a straight lead against the front hook kick.

move too late, you will not have enough time to evade the hit. But if you move at the proper moment—as shown in the following sequences—then you'll be able to angle and avoid the kick. You'll also be in a great position to counterattack because your opponent won't be able to cover his centerline. While there are no set rules on exactly how you angle, JKD practitioners are usually successful when they move at a 45-degree angle away from the direction of the kick.

Angle With a Quick-Step

A: Evasions work well with angles because both techniques help JKD practitioners avoid the power of a strike. It also puts them in a position to counterattack.

B: Shawn King (right) does a quick-step to the left, which requires quickly crossing his front foot over his rear foot. Because he does it so fast, any disadvantage is made negligible.

C: With his body turned away from the strike at a 45 degree-angle, King lessens the penetrating power of Jeremy Lynch's hook kick. He also gives himself the opportunity to take advantage of an open line and counterattacks with a straight lead punch.

Angle With a Step Forward

A: Angling is done even if a JKD practitioner steps forward into the brim-of-fire line. He just steps forward and angles away from the strike. This not only puts his body at a 45-degree angle to the kick, which lessens the penetrating power, but also takes away from the opponent's force because the practitioner is closer.

B: Shawn King (left) steps forward and away during the delivery of a rear hook kick from an unmatched stance.

C: Because he is now closer than Jeremy Lynch expected, King intercepts the attack with an attack of his own—a hand strike to the chin.

When unsure what kick an opponent is throwing or if caught off-guard, a JKD practitioner moves beyond the fighting measure because it's usually his best option. By effectively controlling his distance, he gives himself an opportunity to counterattack. However, if the JKD stylist moves too far back, he negates any chance he has to intercept the opponent's kick. To avoid this, Lee taught that if an opponent launches a side kick, a JKD practitioner should move back just enough so that the kick barely touches his shirt. This allows the practitioner to remain close enough to counterattack before the opponent has time to renew his attack.

Basically, you want to intercept a kicking-tool attack before your opponent recovers his fighting stance, meaning before his striking leg returns to the ground. The following sequences use a side kick, but the concept applies to any kick. And sometimes, you want to move back too far on purpose so as to draw a second kick from your attacker. This will allow you ample time to counter his second kick with either a stop-hit or kick.

Using Distance as a Defense With a Hand Tool

A: When Shawn King (left) tries to kick his opponent, Jeremy Lynch uses his front leg to slide back just enough to barely dodge the attack. What counterattack he plans to use depends on Lynch's weight distribution and body feel (See Page 107.) as he retreats.

B: Note that when you retreat, most of the time your body will be straight. As your rear foot touches the ground, push forward just enough to hit your opponent with a straight lead punch. This could be a stationary punch, lead-step or push-step depending on the distance and the length of his leg.

Using Distance as a Defense With a Kicking Tool

A: Jeremy Lynch (right) slides back to avoid a kick, but most of his weight is now on his front leg.

B: To counterattack efficiently, Lynch launches a kick because his body is chambered and ready to throw one.

Grappling

Although it is impossible to cover every form of defense in one book, it is important for a JKD practitioner to recognize what kind of opponent he's dealing with and act accordingly. Because ground fighting is not the focus of jeet kune do, he still must learn how to get back on his feet after a takedown.

Lee told his students to study the illegal tactics of popular ring sports and martial arts competitions so they can exploit them. Because biting, pinching, groin attacks and eye gouging are illegal in grappling and mixed-martial arts competitions, grapplers and MMA fighters don't learn how to defend against them. As a result, most grapplers leave themselves vulnerable to these attacks during a real altercation. Remember, whatever you can do to an opponent, he can do to you. Also, a grappler possesses far more training and techniques on the ground, so the goal is to get back to your feet as quickly as possible while making it impossible for your opponent to continue.

The Clinch

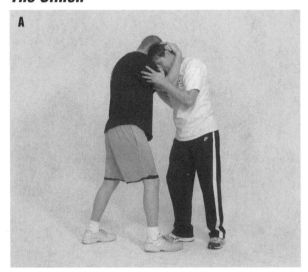

A: Jeremy Lynch (right) is caught in a clinch.

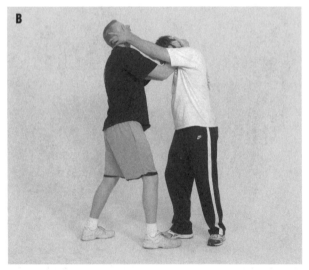

B: To free himself before Shawn King does a takedown, Lynch attacks his opponent's eyes and then follows up with a head throw (not shown).

Wrestling Shoot

A: Tim Tackett (left) faces Jeremy Lynch, a grappler.

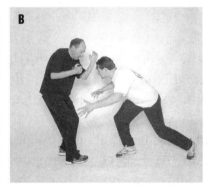

B: Lynch attempts to wrestle Tackett to the ground by scooping up his legs with a wrestling shoot.

C: Tackett strengthens his stance by establishing a low base. He also blocks the attempt by placing his forearm on the grappler's neck. This helps Tackett maintain his distance.

D: While placing his forearm on the grappler's neck, Tackett performs an upward finger attack to the grappler's eyes. Because the grappler is low to the ground and intent on taking out his legs, Tackett knows it's a bad idea to try to intercept the attack with a kick.

Regaining a Standing Position

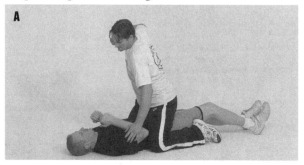

A: When you're on your back, make sure that your head is off the ground, your elbows are tucked in and your arms are protecting your head. The same four-corner defenses apply when you are on your back.

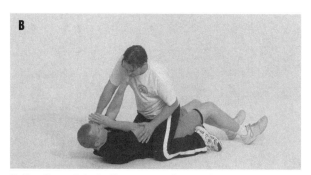

B: Use finger jabs to the opponent's eyes for greater distance.

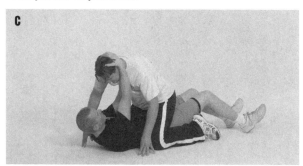

C, D: After hitting him, pull his head down to your chest by either grabbing his head, clothes or skin, and turn his head to the side, cupping his chin with your hands, so he can't bite you.

E, F: Roll him over on to his back while twisting his head. Be careful when performing any head-twisting techniques in training because you could injure your partner.

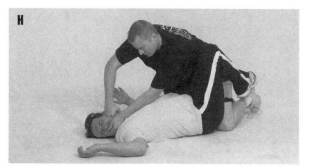

G, H: Finish him and get back to your feet. (Note: This last part is not technically *jeet kune do* because we did not learn it from Bruce Lee.)

Chapter 6
ATTACKS

"Half the battle is won when one knows what the adversary is doing."
—Bruce Lee, *Tao of Jeet Kune Do*

Jeet kune do is a martial art based primarily on attacks. In fact, as shown in Chapter 5, JKD practitioners even prefer to defend against an attack with an offensive technique of their own. However, to carry out an attack successfully, a JKD practitioner needs confidence, accuracy, speed, timing and the ability to perfectly judge distance. He also needs the ability to quickly recover and follow up his attack because, even though he strives to disable his opponent with a stop-hit, he still might need a second strike in a real conflict. But that doesn't mean that the first strike isn't crucial. By knowing when to hit and what to hit with, the first blow can be extremely advantageous. This is why Lee spent a lot of time working on various methods of attack, which is what this chapter covers.

Opponent Identification

In order to know when to hit an opponent, a JKD stylist needs to identify what kind of adversary he is facing. There are generally five categories of attackers:

- **The blocker** stands his ground in a fight by blocking, hoping to eventually find an opening for a counterattack. Like a boxer, he covers himself and waits for a time lag so he can counter.
- **The runner** is an opponent who retreats. He hopes that by giving up ground, he'll figure out his adversary's strategy and counter when his adversary is off-balance.
- **The banger** is an unsophisticated opponent who charges blindly into a fight, hoping to knock his adversary out with a flurry of kicks and punches. His straightforward style makes him dangerous because a JKD practitioner won't have time to do any type of complicated defense.

- **The shooter** is a grappler who is a skilled ground fighter. Like a football player, he tries to tackle his adversary to the ground. Once there, he repeatedly pounds his opponent into submission. (Note: Although Lee focused mainly on stand-up fighting, spend some time improving your grappling skills so you can quickly get back to your feet.)
- **The interceptor** waits for his adversary to make the first move and then launches a stop-hit, stop-kick or counterstrike. An interceptor fights somewhat like a JKD practitioner.

Because a JKD stylist needs knowledge and training to figure out which type of opponent he's facing, familiarize yourself with as many martial arts as possible. Study and observe how other martial artists stand and move, and this knowledge will help you determine whether you have the tools necessary to deal with certain attacks and defenses before an actual conflict. Also note that this book will mainly focus on blockers, runners and interceptors.

Principles of Attack

In addition to identifying opponents, there are certain principles that help a JKD practitioner launch a successful attack:

- *Use the longest weapon to the closest target.* Lee demonstrated this principle during a TV episode of *Longstreet* by targeting a cop's knee with a side kick. By using the longest kicking tool (the rear side kick to the front shin or knee) or the longest hand attack (a finger jab to the eyes), an attack becomes safer to execute. The weapons' range helps maintain the fighting measure, and the target's close proximity makes the attacks difficult for an opponent to avoid because he is moving into the brim-of-fire line.
- *Take your closest shot.* Sometimes people become so attached to certain attack patterns that they forget to target their opponent's closest open point. Rather than try to complete a complex technique, launch an attack at the closest target with enough force to end the fight. If this fails, the attack should set up a follow-up technique that disables the opponent. Basically, instead of following a set attack pattern, flow in relationship to your opponent.
- *Don't attack where your opponent is, attack where he will be.* If an opponent tries to move outside the range of his attack, a JKD stylist adjusts his aim to ensure that he can still hit the opponent with the most snap and power.

By applying these particular principles to your training, you'll be able to maintain a form-less form (styleless style) in which every possible line of attack and defense is available.

Elements of Attacks

Lee divided attacks into two basic types: primary attacks and secondary attacks. Primary attacks are offensive techniques based on three elements: pace, fraud and force. Pace refers to speed and accuracy, and pace attacks—such as the fast straight lead punch—are rarely deceptive. Fraud refers to fakes or feints. Fraud techniques either appear to attack a particular line and then switch to an open line or trick the opponent into thinking that the fighting measure has not been breached. Force refers to attacking a closed line with enough power to open it. Trapping and leg-obstruction techniques rely primarily on force. The book already discussed pace attacks in Chapter 3, and there will be examples of fraud and force attacks later in this chapter.

Secondary attacks—such as a stop-hit—outmaneuver or counter an opponent's attack. Basically, they intercept, which is the essence of jeet kune do. Secondary attacks intercept an opponent's strike during one of five key stages: attack on intention, attack on preparation, attack on delivery, attack on completion and attack on recovery. Attacking on intention or preparation is the ideal time for a JKD practitioner to intercept a strike because the opponent telegraphs his intent while preparing to attack with subtle movements, such as tensing his muscles, looking at his target or chambering his fist. Once he commits to his attack, the opponent cannot defend himself with a counterstrike or distance. The very fact that he is attempting to hit creates an opening. Otherwise, it's best to intercept on delivery, which is when the opponent moves into the brim-of-fire line.

Another important element of attack is speed, which enhances a fighter's deceptive moves and determines how quickly he can launch counterattacks. Jeet kune do breaks speed down into several categories:

- **perceptual speed**, which is the quickness of the eyes.
- **mental speed**, which refers to the quickness of a JKD practitioner's mind and his ability to process is seen.
- **initiation speed**, which is how quickly the JKD stylist reacts to an attack, meaning when he sees an opponent initiate a punch or how quickly he moves to intercept it.
- **performance speed**, which refers to the speed of an attack.
- **alteration speed**, which is how long it takes a JKD practitioner to change the direction of his attack.
- **sensitivity speed**, which refers to a JKD stylist's ability to react quickly when attacked and *feel* a line open up, meaning that through contact with his opponent, he reacts quickly to intercept. This is particularly common in grappling and hand-trapping techniques.

Because it's important to know that various speeds influence an attack, keep these in mind while studying this chapter's techniques.

Finally, "body feel" is extremely important because it allows a JKD stylist to maintain perfect balance, regardless of whether he's in the fighting measure, moving into the brim-of-fire line or recovering his original position. Body feel refers to knowing how your body is positioned at all times. Someone who has mastered body feel never has to look down at his feet to see where they are or double-check his distance to make sure his long strike can hit his close target. Basically, he is always in balance with himself and his surroundings.

To maintain proper body feel, you must be perfectly balanced and totally alert before, during and after an attack. You are ready for everything and are calm in the face of any opponent, attack or defense. However, this requires a great deal of practice.

The Five Ways of Attack

Lee divided how a JKD practitioner attacks into five ways—a concept he borrowed from Western fencing. It's also a good, logical way to organize the techniques found in Chapter 3 and Chapter 4. As a student of jeet kune do, you must learn to defend against all five attacks and use your knowledge of them to know when to launch an effective attack against any type of opponent. However, not all five ways work against every opponent, so it's essential to quickly figure out what kind of opponent you're facing. In most ring sports, you'll study your opponent and his fighting style before entering the ring. Street fights won't give you that opportunity, so observe your opponent's stances and movements to determine what kind of opponent you're facing.

1. The Single Direct Attack

The single direct attack is exactly what it sounds like: an attack that moves in a straight line to the target. However, performing one successfully depends on a JKD practitioner's speed and ability to catch his opponent off-guard. This is because the practitioner needs to avoid the opponent's counterattacks. In addition, if the JKD practitioner attacks someone who is skilled in jeet kune do, he invites disaster because his opponent will definitely stop-hit or stop-kick him. But do note that with any hand attack, the opponent's lead leg is vulnerable, especially to a side kick that aims at the shin or knee. By utilizing Lee's principle of "the longest weapon to the closest target," you can increase the chances of your attack's success despite the risk of a stop-hit.

As a subcategory of the single direct attack, single angular attacks differ in one key aspect: They travel at an angle rather than a straight line to avoid stop-hits and kicks. However, if your opponent tries to stop-hit your single angular attacks, he'll be at a disadvantage because he won't have time to take your strike's angle into account. Some examples of single angular

Single Direct Attack: Finger Jab

A, B, C: The finger jab is a direct forward strike that moves in a straight line to the target.

attacks are the curve right and left attacks mentioned in Chapter 3 and quick-step evasions mentioned in Chapter 5.

Single Angular Attack: Quick-Step

A, B, C: Tim Tackett (right) travels at an angle to avoid Jeremy Lynch's stop-hit before attacking with an angular hit of his own.

2. Attacks by Combination

Attacks by combination are techniques strung together with a steady rhythm, meaning the pattern of a JKD practitioner's offensive techniques is uniform. For specific hand and kicking combinations, refer to the techniques discussed in Part I.

However, it's important not to become bound by other people's combinations. For example, one JKD practitioner may find that he is more effective performing a front lead hook kick combined with a straight lead punch, while another practitioner may find that the combination is not effective for himself. But as a starting point to your own training, begin with set combinations because they help lay the foundation for variations in technique.

Here's a simple overview of common attacks by combination; "H" refers to hand techniques, and "F" refers to foot techniques:

- H – H
- F – H
- H – F
- F – F
- H – H – H
- H – H – F
- H – F – F
- H – F – H
- F – F – H
- F – H – F
- F – H – H
- F – F – F

Using the tools in Chapter 3 and Chapter 4 to do these combinations provides JKD practitioners with a nearly endless supply of attacks by combination. Furthermore, adding attacks not mentioned in this book—like knee or elbow strikes, as well as attacking different lines (high to low, low to high, inside to outside line, outside to inside line)—not only increases a JKD stylist's arsenal of offensive moves but also makes his attacks more unpredictable.

Attacks by combination can also be performed using "broken rhythm." Most people train in a steady rhythm and move while fighting in predictable patterns. Because JKD stylists want to be unpredictable, they usually use a broken rhythm rather than "cadence" (specific rhythm for a series of movements) in a steady rhythm. To use broken rhythm, change your cadence by either a) altering the time between strikes or b) changing the strikes' speed.

For example, consider an H – H – H combination. When using steady rhythm, a JKD practitioner launches each strike, one after the other, at a consistent pace. When varying the cadence, a broken rhythm H – H – H combination looks more like this: H – Pause – H – H or H – H – Pause – H.

Broken rhythm also affects speed. With steady rhythm, speed is usually mapped out as: H (fast) – H (fast) – H (fast). In contrast, broken rhythm breaks up a combination's speed into something more like this: H (slow) – H (fast) – H (fast) or H (fast) – H (slow) – H (fast).

By altering rhythm, timing and pace, a JKD stylist makes his attacks more difficult to read, which is an essential strategy against blockers and runners. When fighting a blocker, if you don't attack at the right moment, he will block your attack. Even worse, if you fully commit yourself to an attack and he blocks it, you'll be knocked off-balance. Basically, the more energy you put behind a punch, the more your hand snaps back when it's blocked, creating a vulnerable time lag between your attack and your next move. In contrast, if you attack a runner at the wrong moment, he will move out of range, forcing you to chase him. To overcome these issues, use a two-hit, broken-rhythm combination against these opponents so they won't know when to defend.

Improper Pace and Timing Against a Blocker

A: Bob Bremer (left) and Jim Sewell face each other in matching stances.

B: Bremer attacks with a finger slice. Because Bremer's pacing and timing is wrong, Sewell blocks it, giving him an open line to counter.

Improper Pace and Timing Against a Runner

A: Jeremy Lynch (left) and Shawn King face each other in matching fighting stances. King is a runner.

B: When Lynch launches a finger slice at full speed and power, King picks up on the attack's preparation and retreats.

C: King is too far away for Lynch to hit with his hook kick to the groin. Because Lynch's pacing and timing are wrong, King remains safely outside Lynch's range.

In the two previous sequences, Lynch and Bremer can't land their combinations because of poor pace and timing and because they are launching their attacks at a steady rhythm. The steady rhythm combination, known as a 1 – 2 combination, that Lynch uses launches both strikes at a fast – fast speed. This means that King, who is a runner, can take advantage of the time lag between strikes and move out of reach. In contrast, Bremer launches his strike with speed and at full power, but because he is blocked, he leaves an opening for his opponent to use instead.

Because improper pace, timing and steady rhythm combinations can leave a JKD practitioner vulnerable to counters, Lee came up with the "o.n.e. – 2" combination attack. Instead of attacking at a steady 1(fast) – 2(fast) pace, a JKD practitioner throws less force behind his first strike. At the moment his first punch fully extends, he follows it up with a second punch thrown at full strength. Or consider it like this: A 1 – 2 combination is a fast–fast attack, but a o.n.e. – 2 combination is a slow – fast attack. Lee's broken-rhythm attack extends the first strike so that there is no time lag between both hits, which means the opponent won't be able to counter the JKD stylist at all.

O.N.E. – 2 Combination Against a Runner

A: Tim Tackett (left) faces Jeremy Lynch, a runner, in a matching stance.

B: Tackett starts his lead step a second after he launches his finger slice. Tackett's finger slice reaches full extension because it is the "slow" strike in his combination attack.

C: However, Tackett throws a hook kick to the groin as soon as his arm reaches full extension. The runner would have expected Tackett to recover his original position before launching another strike. This is why he will not be able to retreat to a safe position and avoid the strike.

O.N.E. – 2 Combination Against a Blocker

A: At the fighting measure, Jeremy Lynch (left) faces Shawn King, a blocker.

B: Using broken rhythm (slow – fast), Lynch throws a finger slice as his initial strike because it doesn't require a lot of power. Remember, he's not throwing a feint or fake; instead, he is performing a finger slice at full extension.

C: Because his first hit is slower than his second, Lynch can mask his second hit. His finger slice is at full extension when he begins the kick with his lead leg.

D: Before King can respond, Lynch has completed his quicker second strike.

There is always a time lag in a steady-rhythm fast – fast 1 – 2 combination because the energy of the first hit has to go through the target before a JKD stylist can launch the second attack. If the first hit penetrates, the slight time lag between the JKD stylist's attacks doesn't matter. However, if his opponent is a blocker or runner, it's doubtful either of the strikes in a 1 – 2 combination will land successfully. But that doesn't mean that a broken-rhythm fast – fast combination, like the negative-one-positive-two combination, won't work, especially against a blocker. Unlike the standard 1 – 2 combination, a JKD practitioner launches the negative first strike at full power and speed but does not penetrate his target. Instead, the punch only hits the surface. To perform one, imagine there is an egg inside your glove and your goal is to crack only its surface while striking your target. (Note: From this point on, the negative-one-positive-two combination will be referred to as a "negative-one-two combination.")

To see which combination has less of a time lag, first hit a focus glove with a full-power 1 – 2 combination. Then, throw a negative hit and immediately follow it up with a penetrating attack. If performed correctly, there will clearly be less of a time lag between the two attacks of the negative-one-two combination. Even if your opponent does block your negative attack, you should be able to hit him with the follow-up because he will not see it. If he does not block the negative strike, follow through with the first strike to penetrate and immobilize your opponent.

1 – 2 Combination Against a Blocker

A: Tim Tackett (left) squares off against Jeremy Lynch, a blocker. He launches a straight lead punch but is blocked by his opponent.

B: There is a time lag because Tackett must recover and prepare for his next strike.

C: Because of the time lag, Lynch easily blocks the second straight lead punch.

Negative-One-Two Combination Against a Blocker

A: Tim Tackett (left) faces Jeremy Lynch, a blocker.

B: Tackett throws his first straight lead punch, but he does not penetrate his target, which allows the blocker to block the blow.

C: This gives Tackett the speed necessary to minimize the time lag between strikes. Now, Tackett easily launches a second straight lead punch at full power that will penetrate the target and be difficult to block. Remember that he launches the positive strike when the negative one is at full extension.

But what if an opponent catches the negative attack instead of blocking it? Rather than bouncing off a block, a JKD practitioner's striking arm gets trapped in place by the opponent. If this happens, transform your negative-one-two combination into a plus-one-two combination. To do this, follow through with your first attack at full power until it penetrates its target. At the very least, your follow-through will create an open line for your second strike. A plus-one-two combination is also a fast – fast attack.

Plus-One-Two Combination Against a Blocker

A: Tim Tackett (left) and Jeremy Lynch face each other in the fighting stance.

B: Tackett launches a full-strength straight lead punch, but Lynch catches it.

C: When the opponent catches the block, Tackett shoves his fist forward to throw the blocker off-balance.

D: This creates an opening that Tackett uses to hit him with a straight rear punch.

3. The Progressive Indirect Attack

Because progressive indirect attacks provoke opponents into using a block or distance as a defense, they work great against blockers and runners. To understand what a progressive indirect attack is, you must know what "progressive" and "indirect" mean.

A progressive technique uses a feint to close the distance. In other words, the strike is a feint that "progresses" toward the target, cutting the distance between a JKD stylist and his opponent in half. The JKD practitioner finishes closing the distance by taking advantage of whatever opening his feint provoked. Basically, a progressive attack helps control distance.

An indirect attack, on the other hand, helps control time. When a JKD practitioner feints, an experienced opponent will probably try to counter his false attack, which opens up another attack line. Feints help control timing by dictating *when* your opponent responds. For example, if a JKD stylist feints slowly to an outside line, the opponent will strike at an inside line. If a JKD stylist feints quickly to an inside line, the opponent will strike at an outside line. Instead of waiting for your opponent's counterattack, the JKD practitioner follows up with another attack before his response. Basically, the goal is to prolong your feint just long enough for your opponent to react so you know *when* he will strike and *when* to launch your second attack.

Feint From an Outside Line to an Inside Line

A: Tim Tackett (left) and Jeremy Lynch are at the fighting measure.

B: Tackett feints a finger slice in a small circle. Lynch's block opens up an inside line.

C: As Lynch blocks the finger slice, Tackett immediately takes advantage of the open inside line by making a small circle and striking Lynch's eyes. Tackett's feint looked like a real attack up until the moment Lynch moves his lead hand away from his centerline. Then, Tackett launches his true attack.

Feint From a High Line to a Low Line

A: Tim Tackett (left) fights Jeremy Lynch in the matching stance.

B: Pretending to launch a true attack by chambering, Tackett feints a finger jab to a high line.

C: When his feint opens Lynch's defense, Tackett then launches a low groin strike.

Because certain feints work better against particular types of opponents, consider what kind of opponent you're facing and the best ways to deceive him. For example, a JKD stylist who creates a false sense of distance, switches up his attack pattern or delays his strike may provoke a blocker into committing himself. Remember, progressive indirect attacks don't always conveniently fit into an intended category, so it's up to you to decide how to use them.

Because a blocker prefers to block until his opponent leaves a line open, creating a false sense of distance may trick a blocker into believing that he is beyond the fighting measure and therefore doesn't need to protect his centerline and four corners as aggressively. Creating the illusion of distance is difficult and requires a great deal of practice with pace, timing and rhythm.

For example, when a well-trained opponent blocks all your attacks, use a progressive indirect attack to deceive the blocker with distance and lure him into opening a line. Throw a full-speed straight lead punch, but don't extend it or put penetration power behind it. The attack will miss, leading the blocker to believe that he's out of your range. If the blocker buys the feints, launch a second attack. As soon as a line opens, launch a fully extended straight lead punch using the opposite hand and full-body rotation.

By contrast, a pattern switch requires a JKD practitioner to first set up a predictable defensive movement pattern that the blocker can detect and read. Once the blocker begins defending against your strikes by rote rather than reacting directly to them, the JKD practitioner launches a true strike along an open line. For example, a JKD stylist repeatedly delivers low punches. His opponent perceives this and blocks accordingly. However, once the JKD stylist senses that his ruse has worked, he completes his feint. As he lowers his body to "deliver" a low punch, he swiftly attacks the open high line with a high rear straight lead punch. In essence, he effectively switches patterns. Proper timing is vital to the success of this progressive indirect attack. Prolonging the pattern too long gives the blocker a chance to get a sense of his surroundings. Instead, maintain the predictable pattern just long enough to keep your opponent from seeing your true intent or punch coming.

Because a "delayed hit" opens the blocker's centerline, it is also extremely effective against a blocker who blocks too much. To perform a delayed hit, strike at your opponent's head to force him to commit with a block and momentarily pause the attack just before contact. This throws the blocker off-balance because he expected a strike with full penetration. When the blocker drops his center, finish the attack.

Delayed Hit

A: Tim Tackett (left) faces Jeremy Lynch, a blocker, in combat.

B: He launches a punch, which causes Lynch to immediately react with a block. However, Tackett delays the strike by pausing just before making contact with Lynch's block. Now his adversary's centerline is open.

C: Tackett continues the strike immediately and hits his target with power.

Runners are a completely different kind of opponent, so the feints discussed probably won't provoke them. Instead, "steal a step" against runners. Because runners prefer putting distance between themselves and their opponent until they can formulate a proper attack, JKD stylists must constantly chase them. To close the gap and give a runner a false sense of security, mask your intent with a hand or kicking tool so you can steal a step by quickly moving forward.

Regular Advance With Push-Steps

A: Jeremy Lynch (right) fights Shawn King, who consistently moves backward and out of reach of Lynch's strikes.

B: To close the distance, Lynch push-steps forward with a strike. However, because of the distance, the strike doesn't land.

C: Lynch must launch another push-step strike to close the distance.

D: Because King constantly moves backward to give himself more reaction time, Lynch's strike misses again.

Stealing a Step With a Hand Attack

A: Jeremy Lynch (right) plans to steal a step with a hand attack.

B: He moves forward with a push-step strike, and the runner retreats out of harm's way.

C: Because Shawn King is focused on the striking arm's recovery, he doesn't notice that Lynch's feet are not returning to the fighting stance position. The deception occurs when the striking arm recovers and Lynch prepares to blast forward.

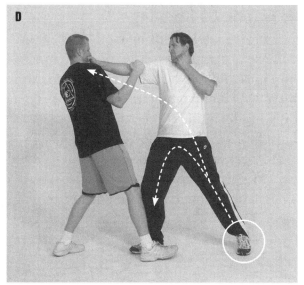

D: This time, Lynch steps forward with greater speed and power. Lynch's strike penetrates its target with force because he is closer than the runner believed.

Stealing a Step With a Kick

A: To close the distance between himself and Shawn King (left), Jeremy Lynch prepares to steal a step with a kick.

B: Lynch launches a basic side kick to King's knee but misses because his opponent is moving backward. However, King doesn't realize that Lynch never fully extends the kick. Instead, he uses it as a cover for a forward step; he does not recover. The kick is similar to the first hit in a o.n.e. – 2 combination attack.

C: Now that he is closer than King realizes, Lynch launches a successful and penetrating straight lead punch.

4. Attack by Drawing

Unfortunately, feinting tactics fail against interceptors because they use attacks as their defense. An attack-by-drawing technique works against an interceptor because it provokes him into thinking he can use a stop-hit. However, because the interceptor launches his stop-hit at the wrong moment, he leaves an open line to attack. Basically, by using an attack-by-drawing technique, you trick an opponent into believing that you are moving forward or have foolishly left a line open.

To perform an attack-by-drawing technique, step forward quickly with a lead step to convince the interceptor that you're attacking, which draws a stop-hit. The technique works against opponents who take advantage of any perceived opening in an attack—regardless of whether they are a blocker, runner, banger, shooter or interceptor.

Step Forward Against an Interceptor

A: Shawn King (left) plans to draw an attack from Jeremy Lynch, an interceptor.

B: King steps forward with his lead leg. Instead of moving forward, King steps up and forward slightly to the left, as if he was slipping to the side of a jab.

C: Because Lynch is an interceptor, he will try to stop-hit King as soon as he detects an attack. By stepping slightly to the left, King avoids impact with the punch.

D: As soon as Lynch misses and is at full extension, King punches back. Lynch is completely open and unable to defend himself. However, this method of drawing an attack never guarantees success, especially if the interceptor stop-kicks instead of stop-hits when you step forward.

Pretending to leave a line open to draw an attack is the most common attack-by-drawing technique. Because the opponent doesn't know the line is a trick, a JKD practitioner can launch an immobilizing attack on his own terms.

Leaving an Apparent Line Open by Lowering the Rear Arm

A: Bob Bremer (left) prepares to draw an opening from Jeremy Lynch.

B: Lowering the rear arm while in the matching stance, Bremer seems to leave his centerline vulnerable to an angular attack.

C: Lynch immediately tries to take advantage of the opening and launches a lead hook punch. He doesn't notice Bremer's step to the right, which will dissipate the power of Lynch's stop-hit.

D: Because Bremer is now at an angle, he has an open line along which to hit with a straight lead punch. His left shoulder also blocks the opponent's strike from reaching its target.

Leaving an Apparent Line Open by Lowering the Front Arm

A: Bob Bremer (left) prepares to draw an opening from Jeremy Lynch.

B: He lowers his front arm, which causes Lynch to think a line has opened.

C: When Lynch tries to take advantage of the opening, Bremer slips to the left of the punch, using his rear hand as a block.

D: With Lynch completely open, Bremer strikes at his body with a straight lead punch.

However, these examples are not the only ways to draw an apparent line. There are many other options, such as:

- raising your front arm to draw a low hit from your opponent,
- raising either of your arms to make your opponent believe he can kick your body, or
- exposing the sides of your body by having one or both elbows not tucked in close.

The best way to work on attacks by drawing—or any other part of jeet kune do—is to experiment with different partners to see what attacks might draw them into opening a line. Then use your knowledge to come up with the best and most efficient counterstrikes for you. Remember, jeet kune do is about taking a principle, technique or tactic and making it your own through self-discovery—just like Lee did.

5. Hand Immobilization Attacks

Many people believe that hand-trapping techniques are the only immobilization attacks available. However, Lee's own notes suggest that he was also interested in foot immobilization attacks as well as hair immobilization attacks. Nevertheless, hand trapping deserves enough consideration that we're devoting the next chapter to it.

Training

Practice the attack methods discussed in this chapter until you know which techniques to use and when to use them. Before combining the methods, master them individually. Once you have practiced all the above, you then will discover the sensitivity to "feel" what your opponent is doing and to flow to the correct response. To accomplish this, train with partners who have vastly different fighting styles until you can flow naturally to the correct attack response, even with your eyes closed.

Chapter 7
HAND-TRAPPING TOOLS

"Nothing bothers an adversary more than variety in both attack and defense."

—Bruce Lee, *Tao of Jeet Kune Do*

Pinning an opponent's hands to carry out an attack requires speed, skill and sensitivity. And even though it is only a facet of hand-immobilization attacks, hand trapping is such a vast art that this entire chapter is dedicated to it.

Reference Points

Reference points are a good place to start learning about trapping because they break down the movements for students. Reference points are markers that let a JKD practitioner know that he is close enough to perform particular techniques. As he improves, the practitioner will be able to speed up his movements to react more fluidly to an opponent's moves.

In *Enter the Dragon,* fighters begin bouts in the matching stance with their lead wrists touching. JKD practitioners call this the "high outside reference point" because it is outside the fighters' centerlines and above the elbows. Because many trapping techniques work from this position, the high outside reference point is usually the first reference point taught to students.

High Outside Reference Point

A: Tim Tackett (right) and Jeremy Lynch stand with their front wrists touching at the high outside reference point.

Low Outside Reference Point

A: Bob Bremer (left) and Jeremy Lynch stand in matching stances with their front wrists touching at the low outside reference point. Because their wrists are outside the center-line and below the elbows, the point refers to the position of the barrier.

Reference Point in the Unmatched Stance

A: Tim Tackett (right) and Jeremy Lynch stand with their wrists on the high unmatched outside reference point. Note: Any time your front arm is on an outside reference point in the unmatched stance, it's most efficient to do a *jut sao*. (See Page 137.)

Answering the Barrier

If a JKD practitioner throws a punch that is blocked, his opponent creates a barrier between himself and the strike of which there are three: the front-hand barrier, the rear-hand barrier and the front-leg barrier. If a JKD stylist throws a punch at an opponent's head, the opponent creates a front-hand barrier by blocking the strike with his lead hand. If the stylist removes this barrier with a trap and then tries to strike again, the opponent may still block it with his rear arm, creating a rear-hand barrier. The opponent creates a front-leg barrier

Answering the Front-Hand Barrier

A: At the high outside reference point, Jeremy Lynch (right) blocks Tim Tackett's strike with a front-hand barrier.

B: Tackett answers the barrier by shooting his arm up and at an angle, aiming just above Lynch's head.

C: From here, Tackett can attack through a different line with his rear hand. He can also use his lead hand to grab his opponent's arm and pull it toward his hip as hard as possible. As he does this, he also hits down with his rear hand. This particular follow-up grab is called a *jut sao*.

Answering the Rear-Hand Barrier

A: Tim Tackett (left) performs a *pak sao* (See Page 130.) on Jeremy Lynch by slapping down his rear arm and pinning his lead arm to Lynch's body.

B: When Tackett tries to take advantage of an open line to strike along, Lynch prevents him with a rear-hand barrier.

C: Performing another variation of the *lop sao*, Tackett pulls his opponent's rear hand across his centerline, which exposes his head and blocks his lead arm. Tackett follows up the grab with a rear-hand hit to the head.

the JKD stylist doesn't cover his lead leg against low attacks. Hand-trapping techniques allow the JKD stylist to remove the hand barriers. He also effectually negates the front-leg barrier by stepping on the opponent's lead foot. In jeet kune do, the response to a barrier is called an "answer." It is only after the JKD practitioner removes the barrier that his hit will land.

One-Inch Punch

A: Tim Tackett (left) and Jeremy Lynch face off in matching stances with their wrists at the high outside reference point.

B: Using his foot to keep the opponent in place and negate the front-leg barrier, Tackett performs a *pak sao*.

C: He pins down the opponent's arms to negate any hand barriers by grabbing the rear wrist with his rear hand and pinning the front wrist to the body with his rear forearm or elbow. At the same time, Tackett launches the close-range one-inch punch.

D: Despite the close range, a proper flick of the wrist gives Tackett the penetration power he needs.

Properly Twisting the Wrist for Power in the One-Inch Punch

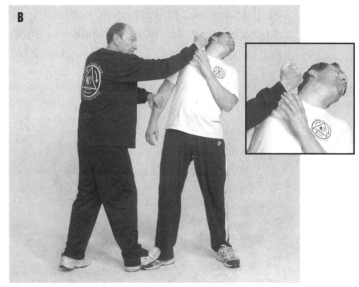

A: Tim Tackett (left) traps Jeremy Lynch's front lead hand with a low inside *pak sao* while simultaneously launching a straight lead punch at Lynch's head. Because he is at such a close range, Tackett will find the one-inch punch extremely effective.

B: Tackett punches with the last three knuckles of his fist, which requires bending his wrist upward to get the proper snap.

Answering the Barrier From the Low Outside Reference Point

A: With their wrists on the low outside reference point, Bob Bremer (left) prepares to break through the barrier. Like most JKD techniques, a hand trap is an offensive move, which means the punch should initiate the technique, followed by the slap. However, a simultaneous punch and trap will also negate any time lags.

B: Slapping the front arm aside, Bremer hits Jeremy Lynch with a lead hand backfist.

Slapping Hand Techniques

In the previous picture sequences, the *pak sao* and *lop sao* were discussed. Like many JKD hand-trapping techniques, the pak sao and lop sao have Chinese names because they come from the Chinese art of wing chun kung fu, which was Lee's first martial art. The pak sao,

Pak Sao and Hit

A: With their wrists touching at the high reference point, Tim Tackett (right) prepares to use a *pak sao* to trap Jeremy Lynch's hand.

B: Tackett slaps Lynch's lead hand away with the first half of the pak sao. He uses his rear hand to pin Lynch's lead arm to his body. As he does this, he chambers his lead fist for a strike.

C: The strike lands. Remember, in a real combat situation, Tackett's movement would be more fluid and involve fewer clicks.

which means the "slapping hand" technique, is the first hand-trapping tactic that most wing chun and JKD practitioners learn. The move combines several actions: a) slapping down the opponent's lead arm, b) pinning the rear one to his body, c) unbalancing the opponent and d) executing a strike. There are three ways to properly execute a pak sao as well as three common mistakes students usually make when learning it.

Simultaneous Pak Sao and Hit

A: Tim Tackett (right) and Jeremy Lynch stand in matching stances with their wrists on the high outside reference point.

B: Using his rear hand, Tackett slaps down Lynch's lead hand and pins it to his body.

C: At the same time, he throws a straight lead punch at Lynch's face. As with other JKD tactics, simultaneously trapping and hitting condenses the time lag between movements, making the entire attack faster.

Hit and Pak Sao

A: Tim Tackett (right) and Jeremy Lynch stand with their wrists at the high outside reference point.

B: While it looks like Lynch's arm will block the hit, Tackett has to move forward quite a bit before it does stop him. In addition, Lynch can't block the strike with his rear hand because it is already halfway to his target. All he can do is open his centerline and try to defend with his lead hand.

C: The hit also acts like a slap because it negates the use of Lynch's lead arm. To ensure that Lynch doesn't launch a kick or counterattack, Tackett finishes the *pak sao* by pinning Lynch's rear hand to Lynch's body, just as his strike hits its target. Tackett also stands on Lynch's foot to trap him in place.

First Common Pak Sao Mistake

A: With their wrists on the high outside reference point, Tim Tackett (right) faces Jeremy Lynch.

B: When Tackett steps forward with a *pak sao,* he fails to block Lynch's front leg.

C: This opens a low line, which Lynch takes advantage of, by launching a groin kick.

Second Common Pak Sao Mistake

A: Jeremy Lynch (right) faces Tim Tackett with his wrist on the high outside reference point.

B: Tackett slaps down Lynch's lead hand and pins his rear hand.

C: However, Tackett does not properly pin Lynch's hand to his body. This gives Lynch enough of an opening to slip loose and counterattack with a palm strike.

Third Common Pak Sao Mistake

A: Anyone who has ever experienced a *pak sao* can attest to the technique's power to unbalance. In this sequence, Tim Tackett (right) faces off against Jeremy Lynch.

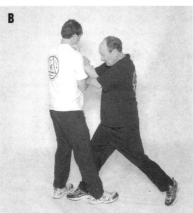

B: Tackett really drives Lynch's pinned arm into the side of his body.

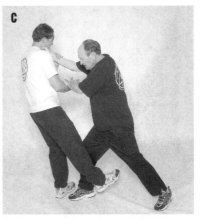

C: The force allows Tackett's strike to penetrate and also guarantees that Lynch won't be able to block or counterattack. That's why you always want to do a pak sao with enough force—without it, you won't be able to penetrate or intercept your opponent like Tackett did in this sequence.

Grabbing Hand Techniques

The lop sao—which means "grabbing hand" in Chinese—combines two movements: a) a grab and b) a jerk of the opponent's arm. It works well by itself or as part of a barrier-breaking combination. In fact, the pak sao and lop sao are usually considered brother and sister techniques because they are easy to transition between, as shown in the section on answering barriers. (See Page 127.)

A common lop sao mistake a JKD practitioner makes is waiting too long to jerk the opponent's arm, which allows his opponent to block or intercept the attack. Like with any JKD attack, it's always better to condense a movement's click count by striking before performing a lop sao. Because the strike is already on the way to its target, the lop sao—which breaks through the barriers—comes as a surprise to an opponent, who realizes that he can't block. However, like with the pak sao, there are several ways to perform a lop sao: a hit followed by a lop sao, a simultaneous hit and lop sao, or a lop sao and hit.

Combination Lop Sao and Hit and Simultaneous Hit and Lop Sao

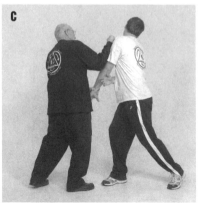

A: Bob Bremer (left) and Jeremy Lynch prepare to fight with their hands on the high outside reference point.

B: Bremer performs a *lop sao* by grabbing and jerking Lynch's front arm to throw him off-balance. However, Lynch manages to block the incoming strike.

C: When this happens, Bremer immediately grabs and jerks down the blocking arm as he simultaneously strikes with his lead hand.

Lop Sao and the Rear-Hand Barrier

A: Tim Tackett (left) and Jeremy Lynch face each other with their wrists on the high outside reference point.

B: Tackett does a *pak sao*, which Lynch is able to block with his rear hand. This maintains his centerline's defense.

C: To remove the barrier, Tackett's rear hand crosses under to grab the rear-hand barrier. He also maintains his lead hand's position to block any counterattacks. Notice how Tackett still pins Lynch's lead foot.

D: Grabbing and jerking the blocking hand downward and over to Lynch's opposing hip, Tackett answers the barrier with a *lop sao* and then launches a strike.

E: Tackett's hammerfist punch successfully penetrates the target.

Circular Disengagements

The *huen sao* is another hand-trapping technique that uses a small circular wrist movement to disengage a block. While the huen sao doesn't technically trap anything, it's taught along with the hand-trapping techniques because it is a good transition technique to use. Its small movement negates time lags between other traps, allowing the JKD stylist to maintain the offensive on his own terms.

If the huen sao is a small disengagement, then the *jao sao* is a large one. In fact, the jao sao is known as a large disengagement in Western fencing. The trapping technique involves movement along several lines: the high-to-low line, low-to-high line, outside-to-inside line or inside-to-outside line, and a circular half movement. Basically, in the jao sao, two opponents stand facing each other with their wrists at the high reference point. One of them performs

Huen Sao as a Transition

A: Tim Tackett (left) and Jeremy Lynch stand with their wrists at the high outside reference point.

B: When Tackett performs a simultaneous *pak sao* with a hit, Lynch manages to block the strike with a rear-hand barrier.

C: Using a *huen sao*, Tackett twists his striking hand around Lynch's blocking one.

D: Tackett then prepares to do a pak sao.

E: He slaps the rear-hand barrier down and to the side of Lynch's waist. As he does this, Tackett also launches a backhand chop to his opponent's throat.

a large counterclockwise circle with his lead hand to hit the opposing side of his adversary's head. To perform this move, the JKD stylist needs a great deal of sensitivity, meaning the ability to feel his opponent's moves through touch rather than sight. (See *chi sao* in the glossary.) If he doesn't, then he won't know whether his adversary plans to block the jao sao with his lead or rear hand. Despite the possibility of a block, the jao sao is a versatile trapping technique

Running Hand From the Matching Stance

A: From the matching stance, Bob Bremer (left) launches a straight lead punch at Jeremy Lynch who blocks it. Now, their wrists touch at the high outside reference point, which lets Bremer know he can perform a *jao sao.*

B: The first jao sao breaks away from Lynch's leading hand. To negate the front-hand barrier, Bremer's rear hand replaces the lead hand at the high outside reference point. Notice, however, that Lynch is about to set up a rear-hand barrier.

C: To counteract it, Bremer does another jao sao to a low line by continuing the large circular motion until he strikes Lynch's groin.

Jao Sao Combination

A: Tim Tackett (left) and Jeremy Lynch face off with their wrists at the high outside reference point. A trapping combination is any trapping technique combined with a punch, kick or other hand-trapping tactic.

B: Tackett performs a *jao sao* by disengaging from the reference point and beginning a large circular motion. To negate Lynch's front-hand barrier, he moves his rear hand to his lead hand's former position on the high outside reference point. This allows him to use sensitivity and feel whether Lynch will attack with his front hand.

C: Tackett steps in, pinning Lynch's arms with his rear hand while simultaneously punching and answering the front-leg barrier.

that is used alone, in combination with other trapping or attack techniques, or as an offensive or defensive move, or even a counterattack. Also, a combination or series of multiple jao sao is referred to as a "running hand" trapping technique, meaning a jao sao that moves from a high-to-low line, or even back to a high line is considered a series.

Jerking Hand Techniques

The *jut sao* is a jerk followed by a delayed hit with the same hand. It's useful against opponents who overcommit to blocks and leave their centerlines open. This gives you an attachment from which to work a hand-trapping technique. The jut sao works well with the jao sao because it is the most efficient follow-up to the large circular disengagement. Students commonly use too much energy and jerk their opponents down too far, giving their opponents a chance to escape through a disengagement and then hit back.

Jao Sao and Jut Sao Combination

A: From the high outside reference point, Tim Tackett (left) plans to use a hand-trapping technique.

B: He performs a *jao sao* and strikes at the left side of Jeremy Lynch's head.

C: At the same time, Tackett jerks Lynch's rear hand down and strikes at Lynch's face with his left rear hand.

D: The jerk allows Tackett to step in and answer all barriers by trapping them. He also hits Lynch with a right punch.

The best way to demonstrate the jut sao is through a basic energy technique known as the harmonious spring drill— a wing chun defense originally used to counter the jerking hand trap. It is called the harmonious spring drill because it teaches students how to flow in "harmony" with their opponents' energy. Here's how to perform it properly: When an opponent

Harmonious Spring Drill

A: Tim Tackett (left) and Jeremy Lynch face each other but their feet are not in the fighting stance. Instead, they are shoulder-width apart. Lynch bends his arms up with his palms facing each other, while Tackett lightly rests his wrists on the two high outside reference points.

B: Tackett tries to jerk Lynch's hands down and then lightly touch Lynch's forehead with his palms.

C: To avoid being touched, Lynch sticks to Tackett's hands. This lets him spring back up to prevent Tackett from touching his forehead. Lynch could also counterattack at the same time with a finger jab by flowing with Tackett's energy to negate his *jut sao* with a hit.

Harmonious Spring Drill in a Combat Situation

A: In real combat, Tim Tackett (left) and Jeremy Lynch find themselves at the high outside reference point.

B: Tackett first performs a *jao sao*.

C: He then jerks Lynch's arms down for a *jut sao*.

D: Because Lynch is using touch to sense Tackett's intentions, he easily blocks Tackett's trap and strike. For the exercise, Lynch aims above Tackett's head so his finger jab doesn't hurt his partner. In real combat, however, Lynch would aim his finger jab at Tackett's eye.

jerks your arm down in a jut sao and tries to hit you with the same hand, stick to his energy like a spring and stay attached to him. JKD practitioners call this "sensitivity" because you *feel* rather than *see* how to move with your opponent. By flowing with an adversary's energy, you can then spring forward with a finger jab to his eyes.

Lee knew that a wing chun stylist would counter a jut sao hand-attack combination with a harmonious spring drill to flow with his opponent's energy and counter the hand-trapping technique with a hit of his own. To solve that problem, Lee found that a jut sao was still an effective attack only if it wasn't followed by a straight punch. Instead, like so many other techniques in jeet kune do, the trapping technique was successful and more deceptive if combined with an angular attack, like a hook punch.

Answering the Harmonious Spring Drill with a Jut Sao

A: Tim Tackett (left) has just finished a *jao sao* hand-trapping technique on Jeremy Lynch.

B: Because Tackett jerked Lynch's arm with a *jut sao*, his fist is now halfway to its target for a hit.

C: Lynch can't stick to Tackett's arm because Tackett uses an angular hook punch.

Jut Sao Variation on the Harmonious Spring Drill Answer

A: Even though Tim Tackett (right) performs this variation, Bruce Lee taught it to Bob Bremer originally.

B: Tackett moves forward quickly to trap Jeremy Lynch's arms. However, the trap will be fast so that Tackett can quickly snap his hands up to perform a hit.

C: Because Tackett jerked down Lynch's arms quickly to make his own elbows snap back up, he's able to hit his opponent with a hook. Remember, to be successful, Tackett uses his speed and snap to counter a possible use of the harmonious spring drill by Lynch.

Second Jut Sao Variation Against the Harmonious Spring Drill

A: Tim Tackett (right) and Jeremy Lynch face each other.

B: Tackett steps forward and swiftly jerks down Lynch's lead arm. The move is done so quickly that Tackett makes contact with Lynch's arm for less than a second.

C: Because of the speed of the jerk, Tackett's hand naturally bounces off Lynch's arm and is redirected to its original target as a strike. Tackett's speed and snap also prevent Lynch from using the harmonious spring drill against him.

Compound Trapping

Many critics argue that combination trapping techniques—like the jao sao, jut sao or pak sao and hit—would never work against a good fighter outside a classroom setting. This is because they believe the fighter will read a JKD practitioner's intention before he pulls off a compound trap, which requires both hands. The truth is that compound traps are difficult to do in real combat—so why do JKD students learn them? The reason is that a JKD practitioner wants to have the option of doing hand-trapping techniques separately or in combination in a real fight. Compound-trapping training helps him to become more proficient in moving fluidly between combat tools so that in a real fight, he can do them quickly, effectively and use them to his opponent's disadvantage.

For example, a JKD student learns how to do a hand-trapping technique. However, he is trained that he can only use the technique when his hand is at the high outside reference point. He also learns this formula: the attacker traps and hits the defender's front-hand barrier; the defender uses the rear-hand barrier to block the attack; the attacker follows up with a second hand trap and hit, which concludes the attack. However, in a fluid combat situation, a JKD practitioner can actually use the concluding, or second, hand trap in the formula as his first technique. Instead of using several hand traps in combination, he uses a hand-trapping tool in combination with something else. This is demonstrated in the example on the following page.

Combination Trapping

A: Tim Tackett (left) and Jeremy Lynch stand at the fighting measure.

B: Tackett feints a kick to the groin. Because Lynch is a runner, he will step backward. Because this is the case, Tackett will steal a step forward to cover the necessary ground.

C: When he steals a step, Tackett comes down to trap Lynch's front-leg barrier and both hand barriers.

D: Tackett comes down as he punches.

Sensitivity

Sensitivity augments the efficiency of trapping. While it can work against a trapping technique—like in the harmonious spring drill—it also can set up a hand-trapping technique, such as the swinging-gate drill. The technique is an energy drill that students learn in order to see how to "go with the flow" in combat rather than against it. Basically, they

Swinging-Gate Drill From a Matching Stance

A: Tim Tackett (left) and Jeremy Lynch face each other in matching stances, with their arms close enough so that they would touch if extended.

B: Tackett strikes with a straight lead punch, which Lynch stops with an inward block. This creates a high inside matching stance reference point.

C: In order to go with the flow of his strike rather than fight the energy of the block, Tackett uses the swinging-gate drill and a *pak sao* to penetrate Lynch's block. Like a gate that swings back and forth on a hinge, Tackett swings back through his strike to launch a new attack.

D: Tackett's pak sao immobilizes Lynch while the "swinging gate" strikes at Lynch's face. Lynch can't use a rear-hand barrier because the energy of his block caused his front hand to over-rotate. This means that by rotating his hips to the left, Lynch makes it impossible to bring his rear hand forward to block Tackett's impending blow. In a real fight, Tackett would also have his foot on Lynch's lead foot.

learn how to react to typical blocks and then follow up with a hand-trapping or appropriate technique. For example, if an opponent blocks with his arm, a JKD practitioner knows not to fight against that opposing energy. Instead, he learns to use the block's energy to create his own advantage. Note: It is called a swinging-gate drill because the arm that is hit reacts like a gate with a spring.

Swinging-Gate Drill From an Unmatched Stance

A: Tim Tackett (left) and Jeremy Lynch stand in unmatched lead fighting stances. Lynch stands close enough so that when Tackett extends his arm they will touch.

B: When Tackett strikes, Lynch blocks to the inside with his forearm, but he could also use his palm. However, by blocking with his forearm, Lynch has left a "handle" above Tackett's striking arm. This is an example of trapping at the unmatched inside reference point.

C: Tackett maintains the energy of his punch by pulling his forearm back to his chest while grabbing Lynch's blocking arm. This means that Tackett is still moving forward.

D: With the front-hand barrier gone, Tackett strikes. Tackett should also have answered the front-foot barrier by stepping on it.

Using the Swinging-Gate Drill in Combat in an Unmatched Stance

A: Tim Tackett (left) and Jeremy Lynch stand at the fighting measure.

B: The best way for Tackett to use the swinging-gate drill to his advantage is with a progressive indirect attack. That's why Tackett starts with a high inside punch.

C: When Lynch blocks, Tackett's striking arm does a swinging gate while his rear arm grabs the blocking arm's wrist. Notice how this maintains the flow, speed and mobility of Tackett's attack.

D: Like a gate swinging closed, Tackett's lead hand snaps back to strike at Lynch's face with a hammerfist.

Deceptive Trapping

JKD students often learn how to trap by placing their arms on reference points and then working on trapping both front- and rear-hand barriers. During the exercise, students trap one or both of their opponents' arms. When they punch, their arms somehow stick to whatever arm their opponents choose to block. This rarely happens in real combat. During a real conflict, there is rarely a static reference point, and the student should be moving so quickly and striking with so much snap that any reference point will last for a split second. A skilled JKD stylist throwing a proper straight lead punch never is attached to a reference point long enough to trap his opponent. Instead, the stylist's elbow snaps his arm back into the fighting stance position, even if his strike is blocked.

To do a hand-trapping technique, some physical connection with your opponent is necessary, especially if you are facing a blocker. Also, to keep an opponent from blocking the trap, you need to throw what Lee called "garbage." Garbage is a deceptive strike that is both heavy and visible so your opponent will try to block it. To throw a heavy hand, relax the striking arm so that it will "stick" to the opponent's forearm and not bounce off or snap back. These techniques work against a blocker and not an interceptor because an interceptor will simply stop-hit or stop-kick you instead.

Garbage Against a Matching Lead Stance

A: Tim Tackett (left) and Jeremy Lynch stand at the fighting measure.

B: Tackett throws a garbage backfist, which sticks to his opponent's forearm. This attachment gives Tackett the reference point he needs to perform a hand-trapping technique.

C: Tackett does a *pak sao*, which answers all barriers.

Trapping as a Defense or Counterattack

A trapping attack usually involves bridging the gap between your opponent and yourself, which can be done with either a simple step or a push-step forward. However, hand-trapping techniques are also useful counterattacks and defensive techniques.

Bridging the Gap With a Pak Sao

A: Tim Tackett (left) and Jeremy Lynch stand at the fighting measure.

B: Using a push-step, Tackett closes the distance with a simultaneous *pak sao*.

Bridging the Gap With a Lop Sao

A: Tim Tackett (left) faces Jeremy Lynch at the fighting measure.

B: Tackett steps forward while throwing a garbage backfist, which Lynch blocks.

C, D: Using both hands, Tackett grabs and pulls Lynch forward with a *lop sao*.

E: Tackett follows up with an upward palm hit to his jaw.

Trapping With Sliding Leverage

A: The most efficient way to defend, trap and hit is by using sliding leverage. Here, Tim Tackett (right) and Jeremy Lynch meet at the fighting measure.

B: When Lynch tries to strike with a straight lead punch, Tackett counters by quickly answering all barriers with a *pak sao* and hit. He uses sliding leverage to move to an open line and avoid the hit.

C: Remember that Tackett's movements are very fluid so the sliding leverage and the *pak sao* and hit all occur at the same time.

Trapping With an Evasion

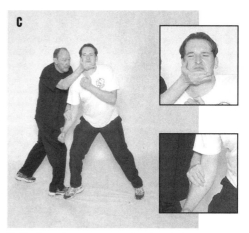

A: With their hands protecting their centerlines, Tim Tackett (left) and Jeremy Lynch stand in matching fighting stances.

B: Tackett uses a quick-step to the left while performing a *pak sao.*

C: He then does an upward palm strike to the jaw, followed by a head turn that can lead to a choke or throw. This is a good defense for a shooter, grappler or someone who wants to get in close to an opponent.

Trapping as a Counterattack From the Matched Stance

A: From a matched stance, Jeremy Lynch (right) prepares to throw a straight lead punch.

B: Tim Tackett catches the punch.

C: Maintaining his hold on the striking fist, he traps both arms with his palms while stepping on his foot. Tackett can then follow up by taking his closest shot with an upward strike to Lynch's jaw.

Chapter 8
SPECIALIZED TOOLS

"Remember, a successful fighter is one who has learned to select, correctly, the strokes he has been taught."

—Bruce Lee, *Tao of Jeet Kune Do*

Some of the best tools in jeet kune do are rarely taught, which is strange because the two techniques discussed here—the leg obstruction and the hammer principle—are outlined in the first 10 lesson plans from *Bruce Lee's Commentaries on the Martial Way*. By practicing these drills, a JKD stylist will come to truly appreciate why jeet kune do is called "the way of the intercepting fist."

The Leg Obstruction

The leg obstruction is one of the most important and useful tools in the JKD stylist's arsenal. While it was one of the first techniques that Lee taught to the Chinatown school in Los Angeles, it is often the least known. In fact, the technique was the fourth lesson detailed in Lee's published lesson plans, and the Chinatown students spent a lot of time practicing it. However, it may be unpopular because the leg-obstruction technique feels awkward at first. Even though the technique may frustrate many students, they should persevere and continue practicing it because it is a versatile tool that can be used for both attack and defense. Also, don't confuse the leg-obstruction kick with the downward side kick. (See Page 64.) The leg obstruction comes straight up from the floor and is meant to "obstruct" the front-leg barrier. In contrast, the downward side kick is a major blow meant to injure an opponent.

Leg Obstruction

A: From the fighting measure, Tim Tackett (right) is ready to defend himself against an attack.

B: Because Tackett has to bridge the gap, he slides up on his rear foot.

C: Tackett uses the energy from the slide to propel his front leg up and out, directly up from the floor.

D: He obstructs Jeremy Lynch's lead leg and also blocks his strike. Two factors make the obstruction fast: a) The leg obstruction doesn't need to be chambered, and b) the rear leg slides forward quickly.

E: By using the leg obstruction in this manner, Tackett creates a situation in which Lynch can't hit or kick him. Now, Tackett can follow up with a trap-and-punch combination of his own. The punch is also fast because the leg obstruction squares Tackett's shoulders and because his fist is cocked for maximum power.

Even if an opponent sees a JKD practitioner coming and tries to stop-kick him, the JKD stylist can beat the strike, but only if he does the leg obstruction correctly. For example: When you attack a JKD stylist, one of the first things he will do is stop-kick you. However, you "obstruct" it with a leg obstruction, as seen on the following page.

Leg Obstruction Against a Stop-Kick

A: Tim Tackett (right) and Jeremy Lynch are at the fighting measure.

B: As Tackett starts to slide up, Lynch defends himself with a stop-kick, but Tackett's leg obstruction "beats him to the punch."

Leg Obstruction Against a Stop-Hit

A: Tim Tackett (right) and Jeremy Lynch face off.

B: As Tackett quickly slides up with a leg obstruction, Lynch tries to step forward with a stop-hit, but Tackett is able to stop his forward movement and do the leg obstruction before Lynch's front lead step has a chance to complete his forward movement.

Because of its speed, the leg obstruction should be one of the main methods of defense against both hand and leg attacks. Here, note how a JKD practitioner uses it to defend against the hand and kicking tools in Part I.

Leg Obstruction Against a Boxer's Jab

A: Tim Tackett (right) and Jeremy Lynch face off.

B: When Lynch attempts to step forward with a boxer's left jab, Tackett's leg obstruction blocks the movement.

Leg Obstruction Against a Rear-Leg Front Kick

A: At the fighting measure, Jeremy Lynch (left) prepares an attack.

B: Tim Tackett slides up to attack on delivery.

C: He executes a leg obstruction more quickly than Lynch launches his kick.

The Hammer Principle

Bremer remembers one Sunday afternoon at his house when Lee was giving him a private lesson on the hammer principle. After being hit in the forehead again and again from six feet away, Bremer asked him: "How can you [do the hammer principle] so fast?"

Lee replied, "I've run into people as fast or faster than I am. I just learned to be deceptive."

The hammer principle is one of the most valuable techniques in jeet kune do and one of the least known and understood. Because the principle is so difficult to do correctly, many students either give up or dismiss the technique entirely. Once you have become relatively proficient with the hammer principle, however, you will quickly realize just how deceptive it is.

The principle is deceptive for two reasons. First, a JKD practitioner's lead hand is closer than his opponent realizes, which makes it more difficult to block. Second, the line of the attack travels directly between the opponent's eyes, where a natural blind spot is created. When an object comes up from the nose to the eyes, a person's vision splits, making it difficult to perceive what is going on.

The principle is named after a "hammer" because it mimics the movement of nailing a picture on a wall. Note: Your forearm should be the only part of your arm that moves, so make sure that your upper arm and shoulder remain still.

Hammer Principle

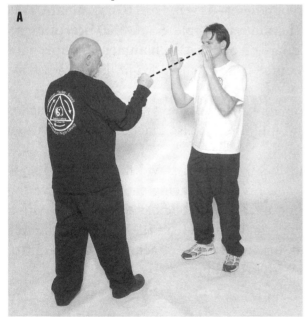

A: Bob Bremer (left) faces Jeremy Lynch at the fighting measure in a fighting stance with his elbow tucked in and his lead hand on a straight line to his partner's nose.

B: For this exercise, Bremer drops his hand so it is even with his partner's chin. Because the hammer principle is such a nonthreatening movement, most of the time your opponent will not be aware of it.

Hammer-Principle Deception

A: Bob Bremer drops his front arm as if he were hammering a nail into the wall.

B: Bremer attacks along a line that takes advantage of the natural blind spot between the eyes.

C: Opponents usually consider this movement nonthreatening and seldom react to it. The move narrows the gap between Bremer and his opponent by six inches, which cuts his reaction time when he attacks.

Like many JKD attacks, a simultaneous hammer and hit is always better than a hammerfist followed by a hit. However, a simultaneous hammer and hit—which includes dropping the hammer while moving toward and striking at an opponent—is very hard to coordinate. This may be why so few have bothered to master the hammer principle. Some JKD practitioners might also believe that they won't have time to square off and use the hammer principle with an offensive technique, like the finger jab. Of course timing is important, but if you have time, you will probably succeed.

However, in training, the real value of the hammer principle comes as a drill, which teaches an attacker how to get rid of his preparation and intention. It also teaches a defender how to read the attacker's intention and preparation.

To do this drill, have the defender stand with his feet shoulder-width apart. His hands should be up, about one-and-a-half feet apart, and his palms facing each other. Have the attacker stand in the on-guard position but far enough away that he has to push-step with a finger jab to touch the defender on the head. The attacker then uses the hammer principle to attack with a finger jab to the defender's head. Be sure that the attacker has good control and just barely touches the defender's forehead with his palm.

Proper Hammer-Principle Distance

A: With his finger jab fully extended, Jeremy Lynch (left) demonstrates the proper distance for the drill.

Proper Drill Control

A: Bob Bremer (left) and Jeremy Lynch face off.

B: Bremer launches a controlled finger jab.

C: He lightly touches his training partner's head with his palm.

The defender then attempts to block the finger jab. This should be easy to do because he only has to move his hand a couple of inches while the attacker has to come from the fighting measure. The drill should work so that neither participant is 100 percent successful. If the defender is able to block the finger jabs, have him hold his hands farther apart. If the attacker is always able to score, have him move farther back. The hammer-principle drill is not a contest; it is a drill to benefit both players.

If the defender can easily see the attack coming, have the defender tell the attacker which movements are giving him away. Once the attacker figures out how to disguise his preparation, he can then move a little farther back. With enough practice, the defender will begin to read the attacker's intention to hit. The attacker then has to get rid of his intention so that, as described by Bruce Lee's character in *Enter the Dragon*, "I do not hit; it hits all by itself" instead. While this may sound esoteric, a JKD practitioner can accomplish nonintention and nonpreparation by spending hours and hours working on the drill.

After doing this drill for a while, work with someone who hasn't practiced it and have him or her throw a punch at you. You will easily see the attack coming and easily be able to avoid it or intercept it. Remember the story about Lee and Bremer? Because Lee had gotten rid of all preparation and intention, he was able to hit Bremer from six feet away. Even though Bremer thought he could easily avoid a hit coming from such a great distance, he never was able to defend himself against Lee's strikes.

Because almost everyone will have some form of preparation when they attack, it's important to know the signs to do the hammer principle properly. The more common ones are the following:

- moving forward with the body before the hand
- having the elbow out when striking
- pulling the hand back before striking
- moving the shoulder before striking
- changing facial expressions just before striking
- any obvious physical tension before striking

Another way to use the hammer principle's blind spot is by standing in the fighting stance with your hand held low near or on your thigh; this is how Lee would stand in demonstrations. When your hand advances toward its target, your partner will have trouble seeing it because it's in a blind spot. To reach the blind spot from the low hand position, bring your arm up rather than down. While it is not exactly the hammer principle, the low hand drill uses the same principles.

Low Hand Drill

A: Tim Tackett (left) starts at the fighting measure with his lead hand on his thigh.

B: From the low hand position, he prepares to strike in a way that makes use of the natural blind spot.

C: Tackett lightly taps Jeremy Lynch on the forehead.

CONCLUSION

"Before I studied the art, a punch to me was just like a punch, a kick was just like a kick. After I'd studied the art, a punch was no longer a punch, a kick no longer a kick. Now that I understand the art, a punch is just a punch, a kick just a kick."

—Bruce Lee, *Tao of Jeet Kune Do*

We've covered a lot of material, and there are more techniques in this book than anyone can ever hope to master. In fact, if you practice the hammer principle enough, you will realize that jeet kune do is an art that can't be truly mastered. While some techniques will feel natural to you, others will feel awkward. Also, JKD teachers emphasize different things. Some teach mostly footwork and the straight lead punch, while others concentrate on crashing the line and blasting. Both approaches are correct because they have the basic structure set by Lee. So while each may appear different, they are really the same.

Because it's more important to do a few things properly than a lot of things poorly, veteran JKD stylists focus on mastering the techniques that work best for them. For example, when a child hits someone, he doesn't think about how to do it; he just hits. Once someone starts taking a martial art and learning a specific way to hit, he begins thinking about how to do it and analyzes every part of the punch. A punch is no longer just a punch. Once he understands the art, he returns to the freedom that he had before learning how to punch, but this time when he punches, it's natural *and* correct.

Bruce Lee said, as remembered by Dan Inosanto, "Learn the principle, abide by the principle, and dissolve the principle. In short, to enter a [mold] without being caged in it, and obey the principle without being bound by [it]." In jeet kune do, the truth exists outside fixed patterns. Some believe this means that there is no correct way to punch and that jeet kune do is merely doing your own thing. What it really means is that there is a proper way to hit in jeet kune do, but if you can find a better way, use it. Don't be bound by the one you know. If you can find a better way to hit with power and with a minimal loss of motion, speed and energy, by all means use it instead.

When learning a technique or teaching one, you may come across one or more of the three boundaries to learning. You may find that you or your student are:

- intellectually bound, which means that you question and over-analyze,
- physically bound, which means that you rely on strength instead of technique (This may work for you until you run into someone stronger.), or
- emotionally bound, which means that your mind keeps you from doing your best, such as worrying about how your technique looks or the outcome of an encounter instead of just "being."

Remember that knowledge in JKD is ultimately self-knowledge. The only opponent you should be concerned with is yourself. As you train, periodically evaluate the following:

- basic fitness
- speed and power
- agility
- flexibility
- awareness
- fighting position
- footwork
- attitude
- sensitivity and deception
- kicking and leg tools in combination and alone
- punching and striking tools in combination and alone
- execution, protection and aggressiveness of techniques
- preparation

You also need to test what you have learned by sparring with partners to ensure that your training will work against whatever type of opponent you may face. As you train, keep in mind that there are no JKD secrets. There is just hard work.

Best of luck on your journey of self-discovery. We end with a story.

"The Woodcutter and the Dragon"
A fable by Bruce Lee as told to Bob Bremer

Bruce Lee told stories to his students in order to explain martial arts concepts. After telling the fable, Bruce Lee would often smile, walk away and never mention it again. He would also never bother to explain the story's meaning, preferring to let the reader discover his or her own interpretation. We hope that you find meaning in this little story.

Once upon a time, there was an old Chinese woodcutter. He was very poor. Every day, he went out into the forest hoping to chop enough wood to sell in the town to make enough money to buy rice to feed his family. One day, when he was deep in the forest cutting down a tree with his trusty ax, he heard a giant roar from the other side of the clearing. He heard the roar again and saw that the trees were shaking as if there was a huge windstorm. Because the wind was calm, he couldn't figure out what was happening on the other side of the clearing.

He soon found out because a huge dragon suddenly appeared. The woodcutter immediately thought to himself: "If I could kill this dragon, I could sell it for so much money that I could feed my family for the rest of my life and never have to cut wood again." The woodcutter then grabbed his ax and took a step toward the dragon.

The dragon then raised a claw with huge talons on it and said, "Hold it right there. I know what you want to do. You want to kill me with that ax so you can sell my body for a lot of money. Well, I'm telling you that if you take one more step, I'll blow my fiery breath on you and burn you to a cinder."

The woodcutter figured it was no use trying to kill the dragon, so he turned his back on him and went back to chopping down his tree. The second time he went to chop the tree, the ax slipped out of his hand and hit the dragon right between the eyes, killing him.

The End.

GLOSSARY

Attack elements refer to the five stages that Bruce Lee taught his students to target during the development of an attack and its eventual defense. The stages are "attack on intention," "attack on preparation," "attack on delivery," "attack on completion" and "attack on recovery."

- *Attack on intention* is the first stage addressed by attack elements. When someone wants to attack, the brain signals for the body to perform the desired technique. Of course, this happens in less than a second, but it can still be enough time to give away an opponent's intention. That's why a JKD stylist really wants to attack with nonintention, which means hitting without thought. (See "nonintention.")

- *Attack on preparation* is the second stage addressed by the attack elements. When most people attack, they telegraph their intended attack in some way. For instance, before punching, an opponent may pull back his hand, tense his shoulder or make a face. A JKD stylist uses this opportunity to intercept an attack before it's launched or, as Bruce Lee called it, to "stop him at the gate."

- *Attack on delivery* is the third attack stage addressed by attack elements. If an opponent has started his punch, a JKD practitioner hits back before his strike reaches its target. In essence, the JKD stylist intercepts the attack on the half beat with a stop-hit. (See "beats.") This "stops" him from being able to make contact with the stylist or launch a second attack.

- *Attack on completion* is the fourth stage addressed by the attack elements, and it refers to intercepting an attack when the opponent's arm is fully extended. This usually happens on the focal point or full beat. (See "focal point" or "beats.") In this stage, a JKD practitioner may also take advantage of a fighter's tendency to overextend his punch.

- *Attack on recovery* is the fifth stage of the attack elements and occurs when an adversary attempts to recover or return his attacking limb to its original starting point. In response, a JKD stylist launches a counter, which fencers call a "response hit." It also generally occurs on the one-and-a-half beat. (See "beats.")

Beats are measurements of time during an attack. For example, an opponent strikes with a straight lead punch. When the fist is midway between its original position and full extension, this is a half beat of time. When the punch reaches full extension, this is one full beat of time. When the punch withdraws midway between full extension and its original place in the fighting stance, this is a one-and-a-half beat of time. If the opponent were to hit with a two-punch combination, like a jab and rear straight punch, then the rear punch would reach full extension on two beats of time. As the rear returns to its original position, this would be two-and-a-half beats of time. In *jeet kune do*, practitioners prefer to counter on the half beats whenever possible.

Body feel refers to when a martial artist has an implicit understanding of how his movements affect his balance and of knowing where his body is at all times. While the concept sounds simple, it's actually something that a lot of people fail to grasp because they don't have a good idea of where their body is in relationship to themselves and their surroundings. For example, if a person steps forward three inches with their front foot and six inches with their rear foot and then four inches forward on their front foot and two inches with their rear, his body feel is "off" because he is unaware that he is off-balance and not maintaining a uniform distance in his fighting stance. In the *Tao of Jeet Kune Do*, Bruce Lee described body feel as, "a harmonious interplay of body and spirit, both inseparable."

Bridging the gap occurs when one opponent closes the space between the fighting measure. (See "fighting measure.") The gap is bridged when either one or the other opponent moves past the fighting measure into striking distance.

Brim-of-fire line is the distance at which either opponent can strike without moving forward because one has crossed the fighting measure. (See "fighting measure.")

Cadence is the specific rhythm for a succession of movements in a technique or combination.

Chi sao is a *wing chun* kung fu energy drill that allows a *jeet kune do* practitioner to feel and/or create openings in an opponent's defense. It is also called the "sticky hands" technique because it is an exercise in which one partner feels the flow of his opponent's energy by "sticking" to his hands and movements. The technique is an especially useful training device for hand traps.

Classical technique is what Bruce Lee believed to be one of the problems with classical martial arts. Because traditional students learn to attack in a predetermined pattern rather than in relationship to their opponents' movements, they are limited to a combination of predetermined moves from their style.

Clicks refer to the way Bruce Lee described a move's efficiency. If a technique is filmed, a *jeet kune do* practitioner can tell how efficient it is by the number of frames. Lee called each frame, or picture in the film, a click and said that a JKD practitioner should try to eliminate as many clicks as possible in his combat.

Commitment refers to how much power a *jeet kune do* practitioner puts into a technique. "Half commitment" is like a boxing jab; it is a minor blow to set up a major blow. "Full commitment" is a major blow, which hits through the target but does not overextend. "Extension commitment" requires the JKD practitioner to throw everything he has at his target with no regard for recovery. This kind of attack, such as a stop-hit or stop-kick, should be attempted only when he is absolutely sure that he *will* hit the target with enough force to end the fight. Note: More powerful techniques take longer to recover from. If you miss with an overcommitted punch, you will probably be vulnerable to a counterattack.

Critical distance line is between the fighting measure and the brim-of-fire line. At this distance, either move back to intercept or move forward to build momentum and get the most power from an attack. By doing this, a *jeet kune do* practitioner gains the necessary power to penetrate two inches.

Deception masks a technique's true intent. For example, a *jeet kune do* stylist tricks his opponent into believing that he is attacking with a high hand strike but instead launches a low kick. Two of the five ways of attack—the attack by drawing and the progressive indirect attack—are based on deception and discussed in Chapter 6.

Defensive movement patterns are predictable movements and footwork. In contrast, the *jeet kune do* martial artist wants to always be unpredictable.

Delayed hit is also known as a "a broken-time attack." To do it, begin a strike, take a slight pause and then renew the attack. A *jeet kune do* stylist uses delayed hits against an opponent who over-blocks. To take advantage of this, the stylist starts a punch, pauses when the opponent begins to block, and then renews the punch as soon as the block ends.

Distracting hand uses a *jeet kune do* practitioner's hands to focus his adversary's attention away from his intended attack. There are three hand-distracting methods: the "obstructing method," the "sound method" and the "combination method." Using the obstructing method, a JKD stylist throws his front hand up to the level of his opponent's eyes while still in the fighting measure, mimicking a progressive indirect attack. This tricks his adversary into thinking that he will attack with his hands; instead he's going to bridge the gap and attack with a low kick. The sound method, as the name implies, uses sound as a distraction, such as clapping your hands before an attack. The third method combines the first two. For example, a JKD practitioner might throw his front hand up and slap his thigh for effect before attacking.

Double time is a term Bruce Lee borrowed from fencing and means blocking an attack and then following up with a *jeet kune do* practitioner's own move. For example, you might block a kick and then launch your own counter-kick. However, be wary because double time is a passive defense. If an opponent feints a JKD practitioner into a block, he has successfully "deceived" the practitioner. This means the opponent's hit will land before the JKD practitioner can muster a counter.

Drawing refers to when a *jeet kune do* stylist tricks an opponent into attacking by purposely leaving some part of his body unprotected and open. This provokes the opponent into thinking that he can launch a successful attack, one that the JKD stylist already has a specific counter in mind for.

Fakes are done when a *jeet kune do* practitioner wants his opponent to go in one direction while he moves in the other. In JKD, there are three kinds of fakes: an eye fake, a body-position fake and a half-motion fake. To trick your opponent with an eye fake, look at one target, then attack another. For example, if the JKD practitioner plans on attacking low, he looks at his opponent's head. This makes the opponent think that the practitioner is going to throw a high attack. A body-position fake means moving in one direction, then attacking the other. If a JKD stylist lowers his body as if he's going to strike at a low target, his opponent will think the stylist will hit low. The opponent will not expect a high attack. A half-motion fake refers to when a JKD stylist uses one of his limbs to distract his opponent from his true line of attack. Basically, it is any incomplete attack that deceives the opponent and opens a line.

Feints are not fakes. They are false attacks meant to confuse an opponent. When doing a continuous motion, like a kick or punch, the motion should seem like a "real" attack until the *jeet kune do* practitioner switches to his true line of attack.

Fencing terms are often interchangeable with martial arts terms in *jeet kune do* because of Lee's studies into Western fighting practices. Some common terms used by JKD practitioners include: "on-guard," which refers to the fighting stance; "parry," which refers to a block; and "riposte," which refers to a hit that follows a block. (See also "double time.")

Fighting measure is the distance a *jeet kune do* practitioner wants to maintain between his opponent and himself. Because the opponent will need to step toward the practitioner to launch an attack, it is also the distance necessary to intercept an attack.

Focal point is the full beat between the opening and closing line of an attack.

Formless form means that *jeet kune do* is not limited by specific techniques and forms of a particular art in which every possible line of attack and defense is considered. It is also known as "styleless style."

Free-fighting technique is a combination of moves that react freely relative to the opponent's moves. For example, when an opponent moves back, you must be versatile, free from limitations and not bound to the specifications of any one technique or move during a real conflict.

Golden principle is the idea that each move must correspond with an opponent's. For example, if an opponent attacks, use a corresponding defense like a stop-hit.

Hyperextension is the farthest a strike or kick can extend.

Interception is the essence of *jeet kune do*: Hit your opponent before he hits you. There are three ways to intercept: a block and hit, a simultaneous hit and block, or a hit followed by a block.

Independent movement does not telegraph or communicate preparation before an attack. It has no intention.

Lines of attack are lines along which an opponent can launch an attack. If kicking above the waist, the martial artist can attack along a high line. If kicking below the waist, the martial artist can attack along a low line. If punching above the elbow, the martial artist can attack along a high line, whereas below the elbow would involve a low-line attack. The inside line is the area inside the guard and centerline, while the outside line is outside the guard and centerline.

Movement time is the time it takes to perform one simple movement, whether it is a step forward or a kick.

Nonintention is a term Bruce Lee used to describe attacking without conscious thought. Consider it like this: When you launch an attack, it should be as if "it hit" rather than "you hit." By masking the preparation and hiding your intention, your opponent won't be able to guess your attack until after it lands. Like many things discussed in the book, this concept is very difficult to master, but it is what *jeet kune do* practitioners strive to achieve.

Pace, fraud and force are the three basic ways to attack. Pace means attacking with superior speed. Fraud involves deceiving an opponent by feinting or faking an attack to one line before switching to another. Force attacks remove a barrier by crashing into it.

Passive move describes what Bruce Lee considered the passive nature of many self-defense techniques. Because these techniques are based on blocking rather than hitting, they allow an adversary to take advantage of the time needed for the defender to block and then set up an attack. This means they lack nonintention (See "nonintention."), which Lee believed lacked efficiency. However, many *jeet kune do* moves are devised around taking advantage of an opponent who only blocks.

Point of vulnerability is when a *jeet kune do* practitioner is most at risk of being hit: during his attack, during his opponent's initial strike or during his follow-up. Be aware that attacking creates an opening for an opponent.

Reaction time is the time gap between a stimulus and a response. For example, the reaction time occurs between an attacker's oncoming punch (the stimulus) and the defender's stop-hit (the response).

Relationship is the concept that you must move and react in relation to your opponent. In *jeet kune do*, this means a practitioner shouldn't attack an adversary based on predetermined moves. Instead, he should attack based on how his opponent acts and reacts.

Renewed attack is the same attack performed twice on a particular opponent. For example, if a *jeet kune do* stylist launches a straight lead punch that is blocked, he quickly renews his attack on the same line. Use a renewed attack when an opponent retreats without adequate cover or if he stays and blocks. In boxing, this idea is known as "redoubling," and in fencing, it is known as *"remise."*

Rhythm is a *jeet kune do* stylist's movement pattern during an attack.

Setup is using a series of attacks to create an opening for the final blow. For example, if you hit low with a straight punch and your opponent lowers his front arm to block it, you've "set" him up for a straight lead punch on a high line to the face.

Sensitivity refers to using touch rather than sight to react to an opponent. It is an important element in trapping hands. *Tai chi, hsing-i* and *wing chun* drills help students "feel" when an opening occurs or when an attack is blocked because relying on sight slows reaction time. *Jeet kune do* has borrowed and adapted some of these drills, but first-generation JKD students who are now teachers stick mostly with those from wing chun.

Single-choice reaction is what a *jeet kune do* stylist strives to have. It means that when someone tries to hit him with a jab, he simply hits back first with a stop-hit. The stylist has one basic response to a single stimulus.

Stop-hit / stop-kick is considered the most efficient method of defense in *jeet kune do*. If an opponent tries to hit a JKD practitioner, the practitioner hits the opponent before the opponent's attack reaches the practitioner. Basically, the JKD practitioners hits back with a stop-hit or stop-kick. Note: The stop-hit or stop-kick requires great awareness and speed to execute effectively.

Time commitment theory helps a *jeet kune do* stylist determine whether his attack or feint will be successful. To apply this theory and determine whether your chosen technique will work against a particular opponent, compare how much time it takes you to deliver the technique with how long it would take for your opponent to react and counter it. Also, the goal of a feint is to trick an opponent into blocking, which opens up a line for you to attack. Because blocking requires a greater time commitment than feinting, you can attack his opening before he has a chance to recover.

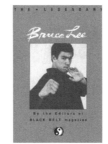